The Girls of Usually

LORI HORVITZ

The
Girls
of Usually

Contemporary Nonfiction
Truman State University Press
Kirksville, Missouri

Copyright © 2015 Truman State University Press, Kirksville, Missouri, 63501
All rights reserved
tsup.truman.edu

Cover art: "Walk after the rain," by Mire Xa, from iStockphoto.com, image
#18725619.

Cover design: Teresa Wheeler

Library of Congress Cataloging-in-Publication Data
Horvitz, Lori, author.
The girls of usually / Lori Horvitz.
    pages cm — (Contemporary nonfiction)
ISBN 978-1-61248-136-4 (pbk. : alk. paper) — ISBN 978-1-61248-137-1
(e-book) 1. Horvitz, Lori. 2. Jewish women—United States—Biography
3. Jews--United States—Identity. 4. Gender identity. I. Title.
E184.37.H67A3 2015
305.48'8924073—dc23
                                                                2014043113

The paper in this publication meets or exceeds the minimum requirements of
the American National Standard for Information Sciences—Permanence of
Paper for Printed Library Materials, ANSI Z39.48–1992.

To my mother and father.

Contents

Acknowledgements

I would like to thank the many kindred spirits who provided generous and supportive feedback on my manuscript, especially Sharon Harrigan, Leah Griesmann, Ann Bauleke, Tracy Bleecker, Andrea McCarrick, Jasmine Beach-Ferrara, and Megan Kirby. For the gift of time and space, I am grateful to the Ragdale Foundation, Fundación Valparaíso, and Virginia Center for the Creative Arts, where parts of this book were written. For their encouragement and guidance, I am indebted to Barbara Smith-Mandell and Monica Barron at Truman State University Press. And to my family and friends in New York, as well as my colleagues, friends, and community in Asheville, I offer you my gratitude.

Excerpts or chapters from this book have first appeared, often in different forms, in *Identity Envy: Wanting to Be Who We're Not: Creative Nonfiction by Queer Writers*, edited by Jim Tushinski and Jim Van Buskirk (Routledge Publishers), *Dear John, I Love Jane: Women Write About Leaving Men for Women*, edited by Candace Walsh and Laura Andre (Seal Press), *P.S. What I Didn't Say: Unsent Letters to Our Female Friends*, edited by Megan McMorris (Seal Press), *Rite of Passage: Tales of Backpacking 'Round Europe*, edited by Lisa Johnson (© 2003 Lonely Planet Publications), *Queer Girls in Class: Lesbian Teachers and Students Tell Their Classroom Stories*, edited by Lori Horvitz (Peter Lang Publishing Group), and *Boomer Girls: Poems by Women from the Baby Boom Generation*, edited by Pamela Gemin and Paula Sergi (University of Iowa Press), as well as in *Hotel Amerika*, *The Southeast Review*, *Ep;phany: A Literary Journal*, *The Chariton Review*,

South Dakota Review, The Tusculum Review, Salt River Review, The Broome Review, The Monarch Review, Compose: A Journal of Simply Good Writing, Burrow Press Review, Hamilton Stone Review, Mad Hatters' Review, and *Dos Passos Review.*

Author's Note: This is a work of creative nonfiction. While all of the stories in this book are true to the best of my recollection, most names and identifying details have been altered to protect the privacy of the people involved. Since I didn't have detailed transcripts and videos of my experiences, I recreated dialogue and scenes in a way to evoke the story's essence based on journals, interviews, and memories, and as we all know, there's a certain lawlessness to memory.

1
The Magician

That's me at fourteen in my one-piece tuxedo shirt, magic wand in hand, my sad eyes focused on the camera. If you look closely, you can see the tripod's reflection in the window behind me. I took the photo. I had nine seconds to press the self-timer button and run into the frame.

Back then I could turn a penny into a dime, transform a red scarf into a green one, and pull coins from the ears of unsuspecting children. Sometimes I performed at birthday parties. "How'd you do that?" the kids asked. And I said, "It's magic," and left it at that. I also played the "psychic game" with my sister. One of us would pick a card and telepathically communicate to the other which card we had picked by focusing with all of our might. One time we got ten in a row and got scared and stopped playing the game.

My world of magic brought me into another dimension, far from the house I grew up in, the house built on suburban landfill, where I moved a dresser in front of my bedroom door because my mother would barge in, despite the sign taped to it: Please Knock Before Entering!!!! As if she knew the precise moment I'd take my shirt off to change into something else, she would find me topless. "Let me see your breasts," she'd say. "Have they grown at all? Where's your period already? If you don't get it soon, I'm taking you to the doctor." When I did get my period at fifteen, she said, "Mazol tov," and gave me a lifetime supply of sanitary napkins. Yet my breasts barely grew. I snuck off into the stacks at the public library and researched breast enlargement surgery and stared at before and after pictures, but I never left the library without checking out books about magic.

Magic gave me a sense control, power. Once I asked a birth-

1

day girl to pick a card and put it back in the deck. I then shot
the deck with a cap gun. Lo and behold, the card she picked
was the only one with a bullet hole through it. The girl shrieked,
hopped across the room, and jumped into her mother's lap. Now
I had more power than the bully neighbor kid who blocked my
path when I rode my banana seat bicycle to mail a letter for my
mother. He pulled the envelope from my hand, dipped it in a
dirty puddle, handed it back, and let me pass.

My magical world was far from all the crap my mother
hoarded: old bicycles, baby clothes, newspapers, broken appliances, all piled high to the ceiling of our two-car garage. Wedged
among the junk were her abstract expressionist paintings created
in college, where she studied with Mark Rothko and Robert
Motherwell. She also knew how to play the piano.

In fourth grade I wanted to take clarinet lessons but my
mother said no, I could only take the French horn. There was no
rental fee for the French horn and a nominal fee for the clarinet.
But I screamed and cried and begged. For a full week. My brother
said I wore her down. Finally we went to a music shop and found
a used clarinet for forty dollars. At the same shop, my mother
eyed an old rosewood grand piano. She bought it. Big men set
it up in our turquoise-carpeted living room and my mother put
her stacks of old sheet music in the bench. Although it was the
centerpiece of the house, never once did she get the piano tuned.
Now and then my mother spread open a piece of sheet music
and played, her long fingers moving across the keyboard. Off-key
piano clanks sang a sorry tune. I asked again and again, "Why
don't we get the piano tuned?" And in response, she hummed the
Israeli national anthem.

I loved the world of illusions, and if I pulled a trick off without
a hitch, I started to believe the illusion myself. Every week I rode
my bicycle ten miles each way along Sunrise Highway to Esposito's
Magic Shop. Among other tricks, I bought steel rings that linked
and unlinked and a magic wand that went limp on command.

When I saw a neighbor kid juggling, I was mesmerized. I wanted to mesmerize too. So for three days straight, I attempted to juggle, first two in one hand, then three in two hands. I practiced and practiced until I got it. And to this day, I have never lost it.

Maybe I took up magic to draw strangers in, to connect with the outside world, like when I snuck in my brother's room and used his CB radio: "Breaker-breaker one-nine, anyone out there?" That's where I met Brian, a fifteen-year-old boy who lived on the other side of town. He had a syrupy sweet voice and asked me questions about my dogs, my magic, my photography. Nobody gave me this kind of attention before. We talked for hours, and I began to swoon. Yes, it was magic, to connect right there on the CB radio, and maybe he could be my boyfriend and I imagined him to look like a younger version of David Cassidy and I could barely sleep thinking about Brian. Before we met, I watched a young couple waiting in line in front of me at the supermarket, the man caressing the woman's back, the woman making soft cooing noises, and I thought, maybe, just maybe, Brian could caress my back like that. I'd never seen such tenderness, right there under supermarket fluorescent glow. But Brian turned out to be a big-eared, pimply-faced nerdy kid, although I still liked hearing his voice over the CB.

Perhaps I took up magic to get attention, to be seen. At school I was the shy, practically mute girl who sat in back of the classroom. Designated as "queer-o faggot" by third grade, my label had nothing to do with my sexuality. Just an easy target. Even Robin Greenblatt, the overweight, almost-blind daughter of the local orthodontist, taunted me. In second grade, she put her big leg up on the last remaining bus seat and told me I wasn't welcome to sit down. She said, "You've got pepper in your underpants, Smelly." When I got off the bus, I ran home and cried to my mother. "She's just jealous of you," my mother said, "because you're pretty and she's ugly." My mother's explanation made perfect sense, yet I still felt trapped. Like Houdini, I had my own box to break out of (or in Houdini's case, a nailed packing crate), the box that kept me complacent in my role as the shy "queer-o faggot," the box holding me captive to deep-rooted patterns, the box I didn't know I could break out of, not until I discovered a trap door for escape, and even then, more times than I'd like to admit, I stayed in the box so familiar, the box that spoke my language, the box containing the lovelorn legacy of my Grandma Becky, who told me she never loved her husband.

"So why'd you marry him?" I asked.

"He bought me a ring."

Magic helped me step into a world where anything was possible, a world where even I might find someone to caress my back. It gave me faith that things would get better once I left home. In the back of my underwear drawer, I left notes for myself: "By the time you read this, you'll be happier and have bigger breasts!" But for now, I practiced magic routines in front of my pocket poodle, Sunshine, the only family member I could hold and hug. In my hot pink bedroom, wallpapered with hippie men flashing peace signs, I performed the Chop Cup trick. I showed Sunshine a red ball and put it under the metal cup and waved my hands and picked the cup up and the ball was gone and Sunshine cocked her head and sniffed, and I waved my hands over the cup again, and the ball reappeared and she wagged her tail and jumped around and ran over to my cowboy boot and humped away, her little black lips in a perfect smile.

2
Shiksa in My Living Room

On the never-tuned grand piano, a two-faced, plastic picture frame held a bar mitzvah family pose on one side, and, on the other a stock photo of a blonde-haired, blue-eyed, busty skier—a picture that came with the frame at the time of purchase. Years went by; still her retouched blue eyes stared me down—when I ran to answer the telephone, when I walked in from a lonely day at high school. Through dusty, glare-proof glass, her perfectly straight nose pointed towards my mother's screams when the greasy chuck steak caught on fire. A decade later, with maroon earmuffs neatly arranged upon her windblown hair, the skier's rosy glow endured, even when our black poodle, Cindy, died of a heart attack in her sleep. This woman became my surrogate sister—my quiet, confident, blonde-haired role model. The *shiksa* in my living room.

I envied the *shiksa*'s long blonde hair. All the while, I had to tame my thick mass of dark, curly hair by using expensive conditioners and spending hours blow-drying it section by section. Every so often I paid my sister fifty cents to iron my mane; the ironing flattened the frizz for a few hours before it coiled back into its usual rat's-nest appearance.

I hadn't thought about why my parents left her in the frame. Plenty of photos could have taken the *shiksa*'s place, family photos stuffed in my mother's bedroom dresser drawer. Years later, I asked my father why the stock photo had never been replaced.

"It was just a nice picture," he said. "And that's where it stayed. No theories, just another picture."

Similar to the shame I felt about my out-of-control hair, I was embarrassed by my unruly family. In restaurants, my father would scream for a waitress from across the room, "Waitress, could you bring me a slab of onion?" Living as if she were a pauper, my mother stuffed her purse with sugar packets, jelly and butter sachets, and leftover bread. From the corner of my eye, I gazed at happy, blonde families (my father referred to them as "The Christians") who spoke in hushed tones, had napkins on their laps, and used them to wipe crumbs from the corners of their mouths. I lowered my head and cowered.

In first grade, I walked with my sister, who was in sixth grade, to the school bus stop. Both of us walked with our heads down; both of us dreaded the walk because of hare-lipped Drew Rosenfarb, son of the local deli owner. Every day, just before we reached our destination, Drew yelled, "There's Ugly and Ugly's sister." At least I was Ugly's *sister*. That year, when I learned about the earth moving at a thousand miles per hour, I asked my teacher, Mrs. Lubell, why we didn't feel the speed, why we didn't get dizzy. She said, "Once you get used to something, you don't notice it." I never understand that answer. Even though I got used to Drew's nasty remark every morning, I couldn't *not* notice him.

But I always noticed the *shiksa* in my living room, her enduring smile, the warmth she exuded from inside the Lucite frame.

During summers, I found consolation at a local recreation program where no one knew me, a free program for town residents. Along with reinventing myself, I reunited with my best camp friend, Lisa Winfrey. Now I was the jawbreaker-in-mouth, captain's first choice for the softball team. I had the dodgeball strong arm, won Field Day ribbons, and starred in camp plays. Lisa and I stood side by side, barbecuing marshmallows, grouting tile ashtrays, weaving baskets, sharing Razzles.

But by fall I transformed back into a long-faced, frizzy-haired, painfully shy tomboy. I did have two misfit friends in junior high band—quiet Christian kids who lived on the other side of town. Athena was dark and Greek, and Connie was gawky and looked like a man. The three of us played clarinet. Right before playing the themes from *MASH* and *Rocky*, we got all worked up and pumped our fists and said, "Yes!"

Once we went on a band exchange trip to another school thirty miles away, a WASPy town with a main street, general store, and big houses on huge plots of land. Each band member stayed with a host family, and I stayed with the family of another clarinetist my age, Nancy. Together we talked about our schools and our towns and our ambitions. She told me she wanted to be a fashion designer. I told her I wanted to be a photographer. "I want to travel," I said. "To see the world." Nancy showed me a photo album from Disney World and Bermuda. I flipped through the pages, admiring the smiling faces, thinking, *Why can't I have a normal family and live in a normal town and go on normal vacations?* Instead, my parents and sister and two brothers and I crammed into an Impala station wagon and drove to historic villages like Williamsburg, Virginia, where people wore scary, old costumes and worked on spinning wheels, hammered iron nails, and blew glass. For me, vacations meant going to boring museums, getting carsick, and throwing up on the side of the road.

At Nancy's dinner table, her parents and brother passed around huge platters of roast beef and fresh green beans and peach cobbler, unlike my family. At dinnertime, we all fought over who got what chicken part, had creamed corn and baked beans poured right onto our plates from the can, and expected nothing more than Ring Dings or Yodels for dessert. And unlike the loud, mean Jewish kids I grew up with, Nancy spoke in a soft voice and seemed interested in everything I said. Although the idea of church and Jesus Christ nailed to a crucifix frightened me, my experience with Nancy confirmed that not only did I grow up in the wrong town, I grew up in the wrong religion. After all, my only fond memory of Hebrew school was riding on back of Mr. Wilkomersky's motorcycle. He took each student on a ride, and when it was my turn I wrapped my arms around his waist and shut my eyes and felt the wind whip against my face and thought, *Maybe this is what it means to be a Jew.* But Mr. Wilkomersky got fired for endangering our lives.

And then I thought Jewish meant chanting prayers in a language I didn't understand, worrying if I had enough friends to invite to my bat mitzvah, and sitting through three-hour-long Passover seders led by my grandfather, a rabbi and retired military officer.

At school I walked with my head down and held my books in such a way to cover my flat chest. And I imagined a day when I'd get to leave Long Island and travel the world and take lots of pictures and find real love. And I always looked forward to coming home, where I'd be consoled by the blonde, blue-eyed *shiksa* in my living room, her cheery expression, her windblown hair, her ski poles pointing upwards.

3
Chickens of Suburbia

One day my mother brought home three full-grown chickens, birds she had gotten from another teacher at the school where she taught kindergarten. My brother named the two larger chickens Mumpy and Measles. I named the smaller one Small Pox and claimed her for my own. Once I cradled her in my arms and kissed the back of her head and squeezed her so tight she shrieked. This was before poodles, before magic.

Every morning before my mother left for work, I stood by the door and asked, "Are you really leaving?" And right before she walked out the door, I screamed, "Don't leave!" But now I had Small Pox to distract and comfort me.

Small Pox and I performed tricks together. I held a stick out and Small Pox perched on it, and no matter how much I moved the stick, she remained perched, although her tiny claws moved back and forth to get a grip.

Every weekday morning, my father fetched Minnie, our brusque black maid, from the local train platform. With tired eyes, a dour expression, and a see-through pocketbook full of tissues and lipstick clutched under her arm, she climbed our front steps and began to clean the kitchen. As soon as the turquoise station wagon disappeared from the driveway, my mother in tow, Minnie whipped the AM dial all the way to the end, to the soul station that played Motown, and we heard lyrics like "O-o-h child, things are gonna get easier," but I'm not sure how much easier things got.

Minnie never mentioned her own kids she had to leave every morning. Although I never saw any segregated water fountains— the Civil Rights Act had passed four years before—a clear divide existed between the black and white neighborhoods. This was the year James Earl Ray killed Martin Luther King, and the day after his assassination, my father took me to the Queens junior high school where he worked as a social studies teacher. His students, mostly African American, cried and sang "We Shall Overcome." I knew something bad and sad had happened but at the end of the day, we drove back to our white suburb and I watched *The Flintstones*. A decade later, a black family moved down the block, and although neighbors talked about the property values going down, they agreed that the profession of the father—a family physician—might make up for his race.

Once Minnie cooked an omelet, plopped it in front my six-year-old teary face, and told me to simmer down. And there the egg sat on a turquoise plastic plate, staring up at me. When she left the room, I folded the egg up like a napkin and slid it under the baseboard heater.

A week later, my brother pointed to the heater and said, "What's that piece of chicken doing there?"

I had to fess up. "It's not a chicken. It's an egg."

For a show-and-tell session, I brought Small Pox to my class. "I feed her sunflower seeds," I said, "and grain from the feed store."

One of my classmates asked if the chicken slept in bed with me, like her dog did with her.

"Small Pox sleeps in the basement," I said. "With Measles and Mumpy."

When I got home, I placed Small Pox on the washing machine and leaned my head down to kiss her. But before my lips could reach her feathered head, she poked me smack in the eye. I ran crying to Minnie.

Minnie stopped sponging the Formica counter and examined my eyeball. She didn't see anything wrong with it.

"Why would Small Pox do that?" I asked, not sure how something I could have loved so much could hurt me.

"Maybe she was thirsty," Minnie said, "and thought your eye was water."

"She tried to drink my eye?"

Minnie put the sponge down and wiped my runny nose with a tissue. "A chicken peck ain't gonna kill you!"

"But I love Small Pox! Why would she hurt me?"

Minnie turned the volume up on the radio and started to move her body. "Forget about the peck. It's time to dance!"

Minnie sang along to Aretha Franklin's "Respect" and showed me how to snap my fingers, but I couldn't get it right. And we danced in the turquoise kitchen, me jumping around, my forefinger and thumb slippy and silent, Minnie gyrating her hips and arms. She snapped her fingers loud and sharp and echoey, a steady heartbeat, and I flailed recklessly, my face a huge grin, trying to copy her smooth moves, and together we were lost in a world of movement, of magic, where we could escape for the moment, both of us singing "R-E-S-P-E-C-T. Find out what it means to me," years away from my understanding of bigotry, years away from learning about sweeter-than-honey kisses, years away from asking for and demanding a little respect, sock it to me sock it to me, a world where things could only get easier.

4

Sham Poodle Dreams

At thirteen, I had a long face and a mouthful of braces, and I needed a friend, a companion, so I begged and screamed and cried for a dog, a pet that I would take full responsibility for. My mother said she was allergic to all dogs but poodles, so I bought a five-pound pocket poodle with money earned from babysitting and delivering newspapers, a purebred with papers, a cream-colored puff that could have easily been mistaken for a rabbit. Sunshine refused to walk on smooth, slippery surfaces such as tile or linoleum, but carpet and concrete were fine. Besides that, she had no qualms when it came to her libido. My sister called her "The Lesbian Poodle." I'm not sure why her sex drive made her a lesbian. Maybe because she scurried away from the neighbor's male pocket poodle, Cricket, in favor of a cowboy boot. Whatever it was, the word "lesbian" meant freak, or freakish behavior, and well, at least Sunshine knew how to find pleasure in the world.

For the first time on television, I heard the words "gay" and "lesbian." Anita Bryant, spokesperson for the Florida orange juice industry, went on a tirade. "If gays are granted rights," she said, "next we'll have to give rights to prostitutes and to people who sleep with Saint Bernards, and to nail biters." I'm not sure how nail biters got mixed into the fray, but certainly she wouldn't approve of a poodle humping my mother's arm. The Florida Citrus Commission didn't approve of Anita Bryant's stance and its resulting boycott of Florida orange juice. They booted her as spokesperson.

At the same time I took up magic, I took up film. I bought a twenty-five-dollar Super 8 movie camera and put it on a tripod, pressed the camera's on-switch for a split second, moved an object in the slightest way, and pressed the on button for another split second. By continually doing this, I was able to create illusions on film—a lawnmower moving across the grass by itself, colored balls traversing in all directions, a line of dog biscuits moving in unison atop turquoise carpet. Once, for the heck of it, I took footage of my dog peeing, and when I flicked the reverse switch on the projector, the poor poodle pissed in reverse. I loved making people gasp. I loved entertaining an audience, whether through magic or photography. My grandmother, who wasn't fond of Sunshine because she peed on her carpet, clapped after I showed her time-lapse film footage of a marigold sprouting from a few seeds. "It's magic," I said.

"Very nice," she said. "But the girls, they usually don't do the magic. Magicians are the men." By that time, I had already learned about women's liberation and Gloria Steinem and called myself a "women's libber."

"Does that mean I can't be a magician?" I said.

"You can I suppose," my grandmother said. "Why not?"

Like photography, magic was a man's domain. Relatives made a point of telling me this. More than thirty years later, an article mentions reasons for the lack of female magicians (still only about 5 percent of the magical workforce). One magician claims magic is like math, like a puzzle, and this could be a reason why more men go into math and science, and in turn, magic. Another said there aren't enough female magician role models. Another spoke of how women, for a long time, were burned at the stake for practicing magic. A woman magician mentioned that women are expected to wear gowns, and you can't exactly hide doves in a gown. Another said magic is a coping mechanism for socially awkward white boys. Yet another said most women magicians get into it because they're interested in performance. As for me, I wanted to escape, entertain, electrify. Although I had never seen a female magician, I was ready to pave the way.

I set up a darkroom in the basement and under red safelight glow, photos, many of Sunshine, magically appeared from a blank sheet of paper. Fascinated at how I could play with light and time, I made photograms using objects like scissors and eyeglasses, and constructed a camera from a Quaker cereal box.

A year after I bought my dog, the American Kennel Club requested I take more photographs of her. They told me to capture her hind and front legs. Although they didn't say why they wanted these photos, I obliged. Later the Kennel Club informed me that Sunshine was, in fact, no longer a pedigreed dog. No explanations. My mother called the breeder and demanded my money back. "Fine," the breeder said. "You'll get the money when you return the dog." My mother suggested I take the money.

So Sunshine was a sham poodle. But I loved my sham poodle and had no intention of trading her in.

Because I took a few summer courses and graduated from high school as soon as possible, I went off to college a year early. But I had to leave Sunshine behind. No pets in the dorms. In my room, I hung a picture of Sunshine, her black lips in a full smile, sitting in my guitar case. Every time I looked at the photo, I felt terrible for abandoning my poor dog. Whenever I visited home, she cried and grabbed hold of my shoulder, her squirmy body wiggling against my chest.

Two years after I left home, I received an early-morning phone call. "Sunshine ran away," my mother said, her voice frantic and parched. By the time my mother phoned, Sunshine had been missing for three days. "I thought we'd find her by now," she said. The story goes something like this: My mother knew a woman whose son was a dog groomer in training. He needed

pets to practice on, so my mother offered up Sunshine. Without
a collar. Just handed her over. The trainee drove Sunshine to a
local college campus where, once the car door opened, my dog
sprinted off.

Perhaps a kind person with wall-to-wall carpeting took her
in, doted on her, and watched her grow old.

Sometimes magic happens without darkrooms or trap doors or
cleverly placed mirrors or fancy cameras. Like in a dream, when
you fly across the sky, arms outstretched, zooming over bridges
and buildings and airplanes. While backpacking through Europe,
five years after Sunshine disappeared, I stayed at a Paris youth
hostel. In a dream that night, I concentrated hard and deep, and
willed my body to levitate. The next night, Sunshine, as she often
did, appeared in my dream. In prior dreams, I would try to grab
hold of her, but her squirmy body always slipped from my arms.
Yet that night, the last time I dreamt of her, I pulled the knob of
a cigarette machine and she flew out. She told me not to worry.
"Don't feel guilty," she said. "I'm okay."

Strange. I never even smoked.

5

A Tourist, of Sorts

During my seventeenth summer, I served tacos and onion rings to drug addicts, people on welfare, blue-collar workers, middle-class beachcombers, and the mentally ill on furlough. At that point, I had completed my first year of college just north of Manhattan, sold my box of tricks to a neighbor kid for seventy-five dollars (now that I was a photography major, I created illusions through my art), experimented with drugs, been dumped by my first boyfriend, and dismissed television as a tool to control the masses.

The day I got the job at Jack in the Box, I made lists: if I worked full-time I could make about a hundred and twenty dollars a week. In two months I could save over a thousand dollars, and then I could buy a Fender Stratocaster guitar and a stereo system and a medium format camera, one of those cameras where you have to look down into a reflective piece of glass, like a periscope.

Because the restaurant was located in a working-class neighborhood ten miles from my Long Island home, I borrowed my father's turquoise Impala station wagon to commute. In my temporary set of wheels, I whipped down Meadowbrook Parkway, zoomed past Jones Beach, while listening to Top 40 radio. This was the summer of Rickie Lee Jones' "Chuck E's in Love" and the Village People's "YMCA" playing over and over and over.

Besides the managers of the restaurant, I was one of only two white employees. The other white employee was an eighteen-year-old, pockmarked, pale kid who dreamed of working his way up the greasy fast-food ladder to a managerial position. Once I swooped up a steak sandwich that had been sitting under the heating lights for over an hour. He said, "Company policy dictates that we throw away any cooked items that don't get sold within thirty minutes." When I sat down to eat the sandwich, he insisted I pay for it.

"But if I don't eat it," I said, "it'll just get thrown away."

"If you eat it, you have to pay for it," he said.

I continued to eat the sandwich, and he ran upstairs and snitched on me.

The other employees were young black women, two of them pregnant with bulging bellies. One day, one of the pregnant girls handed me a mop and bucket and told me to get to work. Ten minutes into my mopping, she walked past, turned on her heel, and stared my way. With hand on her hip, she said, "Girl, you don't know the first thing about mopping. I feel sorry for your husband."

I liked the fast pace, the challenge of taking orders, preparing food, gathering up fries, mixing shakes, ringing up customers, all in record time. Every so often, before a customer opened his or her mouth, I guessed what they'd order. And more times than not, I'd be right. "How'd you know what I wanted?" they asked. And I'd say, "You look like a three taco and a medium Coke kind of person."

And then there were the men from the loony bin down the road, a massive structure overlooking the Atlantic. A big, bald-headed man with tiny, sunken eyes ordered an apple pie and black coffee every day at three o'clock. When I asked if he wanted anything else, he proposed marriage. "I'm serious," he said.

"I have a boyfriend," I said.

"It don't matter. I got plenty of money. I'll take care of you."

At Jack in the Box, I considered myself an outsider. Like an anthropologist, an explorer, I stepped into a world I wasn't familiar with, a foreign world, a world where women my age had babies, co-workers took their jobs seriously and stayed for years, not just for the summer. Yet on the job I didn't receive any privi-

leges. One day, before my three to eleven p.m. shift ended, Danny,
a huge, sweaty assistant manager, followed me into the walk-in
refrigerator and asked, "So when are we gonna have sex?"

I grabbed a crate of lard and waited until he moved away
from the door. In spite of knowing every word of Helen Reddy's
"I Am Woman Hear Me Roar," Danny's comment left me speechless.

The other assistant manager, Melanie, a plump, soft-spoken,
short-haired woman who got kicked out of the army for being a
lesbian, was forthcoming about her sexuality, and that scared me.
Once, when a cute, blond surfer boy walked into the restaurant,
she whispered, "Too bad he's a guy." She told me about how she
met her girlfriend on a Greyhound from Laredo, Texas, to New
York City two years before, how she didn't get along with her girlfriend's mother, how she also had a gay brother. I told her about
my ex-boyfriend, a baby-faced boxer from Queens who dumped
me because I wouldn't have sex with him.

"Maybe you don't like guys," she said, wiping off the aluminum counter.

Before she could say anything else, I offered to fill up the
napkin dispensers.

Every afternoon, her girlfriend, a carbon copy of Melanie,
ordered a to-go meal at the drive-thru, and when I handed
over her order, she asked for Melanie. They whispered and
laughed and finally Melanie's girlfriend would tear out of the
parking lot in her banged-up Monte Carlo as the CB antenna
affixed to her bumper whipped in the wind.

After a week on the job, I knew the Muzak tape loop by
heart: "Bridge Over Troubled Water" segued into Neil Diamond's
"Sweet Caroline" followed by "Eleanor Rigby." In those eight hour
blocks of time, I entered a zone of slippery floors and sizzling
grizzle and sleazy comments, and when the managers weren't
looking, a couple of young black women bossing me around.

A woman from Jamaica, after six months of working,

received a ten-cent-an-hour raise; she was promoted to the equivalent of assistant-assistant manager. She ordered me around with a vengeance, whether it was to scrub toilets or insist I ask every customer if they wanted an apple pie with their order. One day, after catching me lick sauce off the back of my hand while I prepared a taco, she railed at me and my unsanitary ways: "People, they get the diseases dat way!" she said. "Where did you learn to do your cooking, in the gutter?"

My breathing became heavy. I wrapped the diseased taco and slid it down the aluminum order bin and tromped outside. I leaned against my father's station wagon and sobbed. I couldn't stop sobbing.

Melanie found me and offered up a tissue. She paced around my quivering body, asked if I was okay. I kept sobbing.

She put her arm around my shoulder. "Is there something I could do to make things better?"

In the car window, I noticed my shriveled up, pathetic reflection. How could a simple job in a burger joint lead to such emotional upheaval? I turned around and attempted to wipe my tears, only to continue bawling. Finally I cleared my throat. "Why are those girls so mean to me?"

Melanie folded her arms, sighed, lit up a cigarette. "You're doing a great job," she said.

"Not according to some people!"

"Listen," Melanie said. "They won't be bothering you again." She stood by my side until she smoked her cigarette to the very end. Finally she led me back into the restaurant and I finished up my shift.

Ten years later, I sat on a stool at the Cubbyhole, a Greenwich Village lesbian bar. I was sad. My first girlfriend had broken up with

me the week before. So I drank. A blonde-haired, pockmarked guy sat on the stool next to me and ordered a double shot of Jack Daniels. He swigged the liquor, glanced around the bar, turned to me. "It's strange," he said. "I'm the only guy in the bar."

He looked like my pockmarked co-worker from Jack in the Box. Maybe it *was* him. Only now the pockmarks were deeper. "It's a bar for women," I said.

Again he looked around and focused on an attractive couple kissing in the corner. "That's totally hot," he said. "I can't believe I just stumbled upon some girl-on-girl action."

I wanted to tell the bouncer to kick this leering jerk out of the bar. I wanted to push him off his stool and tell him about a friend of mine who got beat up by thugs because she held her girlfriend's hand in public. I wanted to slap his crater face and tell him that my ex broke up with me because I was too scared to come out.

Instead of saying anything, I let the asshole buy me a drink.

When I worked at Jack in the Box, I didn't know why the black girls picked on me, but now I had an explanation: I was a middle-class Jewish girl, a privileged outsider, a tourist of sorts. Like the guy in the bar.

Unlike those Jack in the Box girls, I didn't need to buy bottles and bibs for an infant, pay rent on a shabby apartment, or fight for an extra ten cents an hour. I had no desire to become a fast-food manager. I didn't care about job titles. I didn't have to. Soon enough I'd be back at college, taking art classes, flirting with hippie boys, getting drunk in the school pub. Soon enough I'd buy the camera, stereo, and guitar on my list. Soon enough I'd have a bachelor's degree and get a "real" job, away from hairnets and lard and greasy complexions.

At the end of my last shift at Jack in the Box, I punched my time-card and walked out the door. No farewells. Except for Melanie, who ran from the restaurant just as I started my car. I rolled down the window.

"You were gonna leave," she said, huffing and out of breath, "without saying goodbye?"

"I'm bad at goodbyes," I said, looking at the dashboard. I turned the ignition off and got out of my car.

"Good luck at school," Melanie said, hands in her back pant pockets.

I kicked a stone. After an awkward hug, I got back in my car and pulled out of the parking lot. In my rearview mirror I glanced at the restaurant, the fluorescent-lit, chaotic world I had stepped into for a short while, the restaurant that, when I looked back one last time, disappeared into headlight streaks and highway signs and a vivid memory of my Jamaican co-worker bobbing her head up and down, salting a new batch of fries I just dumped in the fry bin, singing the chorus of "Chuck E's in Love." When we caught eyes, I said, "It's a great song, isn't it?"

She picked up a French fry and bit it in half. "She's pretty good," she said before popping the rest of the fry in her mouth, "for a white girl."

6
My Life as a Hippie Chick

I lived in a dormitory suite with a gaggle of Deadhead hippie chicks who smoked lots of pot, drank Jack Daniels, and obsessed about long-haired hippie boys. We were all artists: painters, illustrators, photographers, sculptors. With my hippie friends, I attended Grateful Dead concerts all over the Northeast. I liked the music. I liked the community. Although proud to associate with hippies and freaks, I was never a *real* Deadhead, only an observer, an imposter. I didn't like wearing Indian skirts and gauzy tops. I felt like an idiot when I tried to dance like the hippies with my arms flailing above my head.

Paula, one of my suitemates, offered to drive us to see the Grateful Dead in Lewiston, Maine—an outdoor show. Five hippie chicks piled into her piss-colored Datsun B-210 and for the next six hours, we listened to Hot Tuna, David Grisman, and Joni Mitchell wailing about California and how she was on a lonely road, "traveling, traveling, traveling."

For the first time in a long while, I didn't feel like I was on a lonely road. I wanted to learn from these travelers, these women who laughed a lot, pranced naked around the suite, and had sex with lots of long-haired men. Precisely what I thought I should be doing. But I was scared. I changed my clothes in the bathroom, or hastily in front of my closet, embarrassed by my flat chest, making sure not to expose my bare torso to my roommate, Janis, who drew sketches of flying carrots and dinosaurs. One night, she drank a half-bottle of Jim Beam and slept with one guy, then returned to the pub and slept with another. At the end of the night, she came back to our room, flicked the light-switch on and said, "You need to get laid."

In the common room of our suite, a bulletin board hung with a list of our names. Next to each name were thumbtacks, each tack representing a sexual partner. Over a four-month period, Paula acquired seven thumbtacks, Janis five, Rebecca four. Even though I hadn't had sex with any men during that timeframe, I had three thumbtacks next to my name. The others said it was okay, since I'd kissed six men. They let the rules slide for me, like some kind of affirmative action.

In the meantime, I spent hours in the school's darkroom, printing multiple exposures of nude bodies superimposed in tree trunks, overexposing a small area of a portrait to highlight another area. Anything but a straightforward photo.

The gay and lesbian organization threw the best parties on campus, and on gay and lesbian night at the campus pub, my suitemates and I bopped to the Talking Heads, Blondie, The B52s, and Devo. We twirled each other around and danced close and pretended to be lesbians. Sometimes Paula and I walked across campus holding hands, giggling. "We're fake lesbians," I said. I loved seeing uncomfortable expressions on the faces of bystanders, the power I had to get under their skin. Or maybe I just wanted attention and no longer had my box of tricks. I didn't think about how my actions might have been offensive to gays and lesbians, how gays and lesbians had to endure uncomfortable reactions, at best, on a daily basis, even at a small liberal arts college just north of Manhattan. This was the year Billie Jean King's ex-lover filed a palimony suit. King called the affair a "mistake" and stayed deep in the closet.

That winter Paula and I traveled to Key West. One night we had gone to Ernest Hemingway's hangout, Sloppy Joe's, and we both got pretty sloppy and found guys to kiss and buy us drinks. Hours later, I wanted to leave. But Paula wasn't ready to end the night. Since she had the car, she dragged me back to a shack owned by J. D., a drunken boat captain with laryngitis. I slept in his living room on a pullout couch with J. D.'s mutt, Shithead.

Afterwards, Paula said, "I gave him a satisfying time, and with that in mind, I'm satisfied."

The day after Sloppy Joe's, Paula and I wrote in our journals, *Where will we be in five years?* Paula wrote, *Living high on a ridge-top with a long-haired man who owns an old Ford pickup truck with a dog in the back. He's wearing overalls with no shirt on underneath, a blue bandana around his neck. We're carpenter partners and do lots of drawings on the side. I'll be very happy. Won't compromise.*

Reality: Five years later, Paula made sculptures using neon lights and ran a vintage-clothing shop in Santa Cruz with her boyfriend, Barry, who fifteen years later would be dead of AIDS.

Me: *I'll live in a small home with enough land to get away from neighbors. Married to a Kenny Loggins-type musician and jam a lot. Have a jeep and travel. Perform on occasion in bars.*

Reality: I lived in a Lower East Side tenement flat and occasionally played and sang in bars. I traveled to Russia and China and many parts of Europe. I told friends that Joseph was still my boyfriend but secretly dated Amy, the aspiring opera singer who worked making keys at a locksmith shop. I didn't know if I was really a lesbian. When Amy tried to hold my hand, I pulled it away. "We'll get killed," I said. "Gay-bashed."

7
Deathbed Pearls

Like me, Luke was eighteen. Like me, Luke played guitar. Like me, Luke wrote bad poetry. But unlike me, Luke was serving time in a correctional facility. Intrigued by this mysterious Californian, I carefully read his chicken-scratch writing and studied the photo he included in his letter—a skinny blonde-haired, blue-eyed boy playing the guitar. I showed a friend who lived down the hall. "He looks like Sean Cassidy!" she said, a jealous tinge to her voice. He sort of did look like Sean Cassidy, without the bad skin. I pinned Luke's picture up on my bulletin board next to a picture of my white pocket poodle and a ticket stub from a Kenny Loggins concert.

A month before, I flipped through the classified section of *Rolling Stone*. An ad caught my eye: "Free Pen Pals From All Over the World!" Since I couldn't travel the world, maybe the world could travel to me. I sent in my name and age and, a week later, received a letter from the pen pal company. For a ten-dollar fee, they'd send me a list of pen pals. *Forget that! I ought to complain to the attorney general for false advertising!* Yet a few days later, tissue-thin airmail letters arrived from India, Brazil, Japan. All written by lonely men wanting a young, American girlfriend. Even though I attended a college where females outnumbered males, I wasn't that desperate.

And then I received Luke's letter.

I sent him a photo of myself playing the guitar, and he responded, "You're more beautiful than I imagined." After a few weeks of written letters, I asked Luke if he had access to a cassette recorder. This was before Internet dating or text messaging. Eight-track tapes were on their way out, but not totally.

And thus we began to record our letters. Luke, originally from Alabama, had a thick Southern accent. When I popped the cassette in the player, his romantic and foreign drawl gave life to his image. Like magic. We talked about our families, music we liked, our goals in life. I sang him original songs, songs I wouldn't dare play for anyone else.

I felt safe with Luke. And he told me how talented and smart and beautiful I was. "And one more thing," he added at the end of one of his tapes. "I think I'm falling in love with you." I didn't respond to the falling-in-love part of the tape, but, I had to admit, I liked it. At school I got drunk and kissed boys (and usually ran away if they tried anything else), but none of them took an interest in my music or art or me the way Luke did.

I finally worked up the nerve to ask Luke why he was serving time. "Drugs," he said. "Got caught with two pounds of marijuana."

Poor kid. What bad luck! After all, my friend Teri brought back pounds of marijuana from New York on a weekly basis. With her hallway door wide open, she weighed out her stash on a scale and packed Baggies, never concerned about breaking laws or going to prison.

In one tape, Luke told me he got into a brawl; his jaw broke and had to be wired back together. "It hurts like hell," he mumbled. "But just thinkin' of you makes the pain easier to swallow."

How could this loving man-boy, the boy who sang me romantic songs and wrote poetry about roses and sunsets, how could he have been violent?

In the meantime, my friends at school asked if Luke could hook them up with their own cute prison pen pals. He was happy to oblige. Perhaps each address he divvied out earned him some clout—some money or cigarettes in a place where the idea of a sexy college girl could go a long way. Within a week, four of my friends began to correspond with four of Luke's prison-mates.

I never went to a high school prom; I always felt like an

outsider, but now I felt like I belonged to an exclusive club. In the cafeteria, my friends gave me updates on their men; they shared pictures they received, the intimate stories of screwed-up families and foster care. "My prison pal comes from San Francisco," one friend told me. "He says when he gets out, he'll show me around and take me to the redwood forest." Another friend passed around a picture of a chisel-faced, dark-haired boy holding a basketball. "He used to be a model," she said, "for the Sears Roebuck catalogue."

A month into her correspondence, another friend received a pearl necklace in the mail. Her prison pen pal told her that his mother gave him the necklace on her deathbed, and he should give it to the woman he loved. My friend, let's call her Shelly, wore the necklace with pride, as if it were a war medal she earned for a heroic act. She caressed the deathbed pearls, reminding herself and others, I suppose, that yes, she was capable of being loved and loving another. Shelly and her prison pal wrote letters to each other every day. In one letter to Shelly, her prison pal mentioned that Luke had a big, black boyfriend, a guy he slept with for protection.

"*My* Luke?" I said.

She fingered her pearls. "Don't tell him I told you."

The next time I recorded a letter to Luke, I couldn't help but mention the rumor of the boyfriend. "It upset me to think your friend would be spreading lies about you," I said.

Luke, angered by the accusation, categorically denied it. "I'm a full-blooded, straight man!" he declared

Shelly's prison pal found out that Shelly told me about the big black man, and that I told Luke, and that Luke confronted Shelly's man, and Shelly's man confronted Shelly, and as a result, she stopped talking to me.

My other friend learned from her Sears Roebuck prisoner that Luke was in the slammer for armed robbery and involuntary manslaughter, not drugs.

Spring was in the air and things got messy, between my friends and between the guys in prison. And then I got a message from Luke: "I'm planning to leave this hellhole by summer's end, and the first thing I want to do is visit you."

The possibility of meeting Luke scared me. Did I really want to ruin my fantasy and meet a wire-jawed criminal?

I took longer and longer to respond to Luke's letters. Eventually our communication died. Within six months, all correspondence between my friends and their prison pals ceased. Shelly forgave me.

Twenty years later, my father emptied out his storage space and sent me boxes of art supplies and books from my college days. In the bottom of one box, I found Luke's tapes bundled together with a dried-out rubber band. I popped a tape in my old cassette player, and Luke's warbled voice echoed from my speakers: "Lori, this is for you," he said. He sang a song about the moon and love and ponies. It was awful.

That same day, I emailed Shelly and asked what she remembered about that time. She wrote:

> I DEFINITELY remember our prison pals! Yours was named Luke, and we called him Lurch. And you sent him tape recordings in this sexy voice, and all the prison pals fell in love with you. Mine sent me this crappy necklace that his mom had given him on her deathbed and made him promise to give it to his future wife, and he sent it to me after like one exchanged letter. It completely creeped me out, and I never wrote back. Nor did I send the necklace back, though it was kind of Cracker Jack-toy quality. I couldn't quite figure out for myself whether his line was genuine or these prison dudes have a racket going. And then I read some article in *Psychology Today* about these pathetic women who fall in love with their prison

pals because they can't handle real relationships, and the whole dynamic gave me the willies. I could just imagine them all, semi-illiterate and bored out of their minds, masturbating to letters from girls they'd never met. Yich.

Perhaps everything about our prison pals was bogus, an illusion, but back in college, I don't remember Shelly doubting the authenticity of those pearls. And I never doubted Luke's words. In fact, before we left college for that summer, I tapped on Shelly's door. She had just begun to pack. "I didn't realize how much crap I have," she said. We talked about our summer plans. She had a camp counselor job lined up; I was on my way to Israel to work on a farm. On her bed, she rolled up a pile of posters and once she had them in a tight roll, she pointed to her dresser and asked me to get her a piece of masking tape. Next to the roll of tape, the pearl necklace spilled from her jewelry box—little sparkly teeth smiling at how the room had fallen quiet.

8
My People

A week before my flight to Tel Aviv, the Israeli military bombed a suspected nuclear reactor in Iraq. My parents insisted I cancel the trip, but why let a little Middle Eastern tension ruin my plans? At nineteen, I was a rebel, a long way from that shy girl in the Long Island hot pink bedroom. To prove it, I shaved stripes into my hairy legs—vertical stripes in one leg, horizontal in the other.

In exchange for free room and board, I chopped vegetables and hoed weeds and mopped floors on a kibbutz—an Israeli collective community—located just outside Nazareth. Every night I partied with blond Danes, a British man from Manchester, a couple of wild-eyed Swiss Germans, and two university girls from Dijon, France. How exciting to bond with young, hip foreigners, to be accepted by a group of people who spoke different languages and had beautiful complexions. At night we drank brandy and White Russians, and on my guitar I played Joni Mitchell, Bonnie Raitt, and Rickie Lee Jones songs. I managed to get to work by seven a.m., but some of the Europeans showed up late, if at all.

Johanna, a twenty-five-year-old ex-junkie from Denmark, had studied music at Copenhagen University. Every now and then, we snuck into the music room at the kibbutz school and Johanna would sit at the piano and take a deep breath as if beginning a recital. She swept her long fingers across the keyboard and played pieces by Chopin, Bach, and Vivaldi.

I had never met a woman like Johanna. She spoke up for herself, could get any man she wanted, was smart, talented, and glamorous in a young Katherine Hepburn movie-star kind of way. She told me she had worked as a prostitute in Copenhagen.

"It started when I needed to support my addiction," she said. Yet Johanna had no shame. In fact, her clientele included politicians, rock stars, and businessmen. Two months before I met her, she had organized a rally with other sex workers in hopes of decriminalizing prostitution. She was the first woman I met who embraced the word "feminist." In college, I heard the word bandied about but pushed it aside, choosing instead to hang around with hippie boys who were threatened by the term.

Three weeks into her stay, Johanna challenged the manager, a Holocaust survivor, when he gave her the task of shelling peas. "Why do the men get the good jobs outside?" she asked. "Why do they get to use dynamite and blow up mines?"

"This is our home and you are our guest," he said. "If you don't like your job, you can leave."

Johanna left. But before she departed, we made plans to meet up in Crete.

The manager called me into his office. "We judge a person by the people they choose to befriend," he said. "You're a nice Jewish girl. You need to think about who you associate with. You need to be with your own people."

Who were my people? In college, I befriended hippies and artists. All outsiders. I've always gravitated towards outsiders. And outsiders have always gravitated towards me.

At this kibbutz started by German Holocaust survivors, I couldn't connect with the Jewish volunteers from the United States. They reminded me of the kids I grew up with, the kids who picked on me or watched me get picked on, when I had no confidence, the straight and narrow kids who studied for the SAT and bragged about their scores on the bus.

Besides, I had fun hanging out with the drunk Europeans. And I didn't think Johanna was so bad. At least she had the guts to speak up.

While walking back to my room at night, I lost my way and stumbled upon one bomb shelter after the next. The loud fighter planes frightened me. An Israeli woman said that the sound of fighter planes comforted her.

I left the kibbutz and stepped onto a gigantic ship bound for Greece. Foghorns blew and we pulled out of Haifa's port. Disheveled hippies spread out sleeping bags and backpacks on the deck. We didn't have the money or need for private berths. I set up my sleeping bag near a beautiful blond man in white genie pants, a tiny turquoise earring in his left ear. He squirted a tube of something pink onto a big round cracker and looked off in the distance. I sat on my knees and asked him, even though I already knew, when we'd arrive in Crete. He put his cracker down, dug inside his backpack, and pulled out a schedule. His index finger moved across the page. He told me we'd arrive tomorrow afternoon. A Dutchman from Amsterdam, he was on his way home to finish his last year of university. For the past three months he had worked out in the fields of another kibbutz. "I'm usually not this dark," he said, studying his tanned arm.

I stretched my goose-bumped, whiter arm out next to his.

That evening, we shared our food and pooled our money to buy a bottle of wine. We stood by the railing and watched the ocean's waves swirling and pounding against the ship. We talked about politics and travel and our studies, and when the sun went down, I saw its reflection in the Dutchman's eyes.

We went back to our bedroom—the deck—and I pulled out my guitar and played the blues and a big crowd gathered and applauded and begged for more. But I already had the groupie I wanted, the Dutchman. After everyone went to bed, he wiggled close to me in his sleeping bag and held me, and I thought, this is magic—a beautiful man, a ship on its way to Greece, a Van Gogh starry night.

When we arrived at Iraklion, Crete's port, the Dutchman followed me off the boat and Johanna waved me over, a huge smile on her face, the gap in her front teeth exposed. She led us to a youth hostel. In the common area, a television blared live coverage of Prince Charles and Lady Diana's royal wedding. No one paid attention.

The next day, we set out for a "nude hippie beach," as Joanna described it. We took bus after bus, the Dutchman always carrying my guitar. After a final two-kilometer walk, we arrived at a tucked-away beach dotted with naked hippies and bonfires. We claimed a small cove, our home for the week. Johanna showed us how to make pita bread from flour and water and rolled out with a wine bottle. Over a bonfire, Joanna talked about the need to speak up, to believe in yourself, to follow your heart. "Because I did," she said, "now sex workers have legal rights in Denmark."

I looked down. "You're so *strong!*"

"You are too!" she said. "You're beautiful. Talented. You will be famous!"

After a week of pita bread and bonfires and watching the sunset over the ocean, we took a ship to Athens, where we visited ruins, ate fresh salads, *souvlaki*, and swigged *ouzo*. The three of us then caught a twenty-four hour bus ride to Istanbul—one long ride of hairpin turns and unpaved, decrepit roads. Without a toilet to speak of. When everyone was fast asleep, I peed into a plastic bag and threw it out the window.

In Istanbul, along with two Englishmen we met along the way, we negotiated with a hotel owner to sleep on his roof for the equivalent of fifty cents a night. A panorama of mosques and minarets encircled us, but at street level, soldiers with machine guns stood on every corner. Turkey was under military dictatorship.

When we explored the city, men stopped and stared—a curious stare without expression. Western woman were a novelty. Often I brought my camera up to eye level and snapped pictures of the men; still they never changed their blank expressions.

One morning, after the others had left the roof, the Dutchman and I remained under our sleeping bags. For the first time, we shed our clothes and fumbled atop each other, our bodies sweaty. To my surprise, the twenty-one-year-old Dutchman seemed unsure of himself. I lightened the mood, made him laugh by reminding him of the caged German shepherds we saw at the pitiful Istanbul zoo the day before.

With our arms loosely wrapped around each other, I heard a cough. There stood two Turkish boys, no more than ten years of age, their arms folded, leaning on the roof's ledge, maybe thirty feet away, staring as if they were watching an action movie. Even after my eyes met theirs, they didn't flinch.

The Dutchman hid under the covers, embarrassed, invaded.

It could have been the foreign country, the foreign man, the foreign circumstance, but I didn't feel mortified. Or maybe it was because I'd seen Johanna in action, fearless, beautiful, unconcerned with what other people thought. She was "my people."

I picked up my camera and took a picture of the boys, as if it were a gun, a shield, a magical device to poof away the foreign eyes glued to my body.

They stared, expressionless, like the men on the street. They continued to stare until they got bored and walked away.

9
A Hushed Blue Underworld

Unlike other arty middle-class friends I made at the small state college I attended, Jessie came from a working-class background. For Jessie, a bastard child enrolled in a federally funded program for disadvantaged students, college was a place to escape from the burden of family life, a reason to quit her full-time customer service job at J. C. Penney, a ticket to a better life than her mother had, all paid in full by Uncle Sam.

Although she had no pretenses of being an artist, she fit right in with the spiky-haired dancers and hip film guys who wore thick, black glasses and knew all the lyrics to Elvis Costello songs. Jessie—pale-skinned with henna-red hair—had a tendency to barge into campus apartments of people she knew and scream, "You be fugly!" before slamming the door shut and running away.

Senior year of college, I lived in an apartment with a working phone line, even though no one ordered service. My roommates and friends took advantage of this complimentary line. My Ecuadorian roommate curled up in a chair and spent whole evenings talking to family in Quito, my roommate's boyfriend often phoned Finland, and Jessie spent hours on the phone chatting with her heroin-addict boyfriend and pregnant mother, both living in nearby Yonkers.

Instead of always running after her obligatory "You be fugly" rant, Jessie began to stay for a while. One day I showed her my latest art project: sepia-toned transparencies of nude women in the school's locker-room shower. Jessie inspected each image with the eye of a jeweler. Before lifting her gaze off the last image, she inquired about Joseph, my boyfriend who attended a college three hours north. "How's the sex?"

I looked downward, felt my face turn red. "It's good."
Jessie lightly slapped my shoulder and cackled. "You're such a prude!"

"How good is it with you and *your boyfriend*?" I asked, focusing on the little birthmark just above her lip.

Jessie gathered the photos in a neat pile and handed them back to me. "It's all right," she mumbled, her eyes fixed on the top photo of a lean-bodied woman lathering her hair. "That's my favorite."

Although she made me nervous—I stumbled over words and occasionally bumped into walls in her presence—I felt like a rock star around Jessie. When I talked, she stared into my eyes and listened, whether it was about my family poodle that got mauled to death by a Great Dane at a Veteran's Day Parade, or my art history paper about Jackson Pollack. She told me about her mother who had a bevy of children by different fathers. On weekends, she would take a bus back to Yonkers and help out with the kids. The concept of someone's mother who kept having kids was foreign to me. But somehow Jessie made light of it, even laughed about it.

One day, and it happened to be my twentieth birthday, I suggested we join the campus food co-op. "Instead of working three hours a month for our membership," I said, "we could make a cake. And the co-op could sell slices of the cake and make a killing."

Jessie wasn't exactly a food-co-op kind of girl. She often mentioned her cravings for a Big Mac and fries. But she came along for the ride. On the ground floor of the student union, I gathered the ingredients needed to make carob cake: eggs, carob, flour, butter, baking power. I asked Jessie if I needed anything else.

She laughed. "I can't even boil an egg!"

Back at my campus apartment, Jessie plopped herself down and phoned her mother. I enjoyed Jessie's presence. And I didn't mind making the cake by myself. Besides, only one person could comfortably fit in my alcove-kitchen. So I cracked eggs and

melted butter and stirred up a batter that looked gooey and choc-
olaty. I then poured the batter into an elongated cake pan and slid
it in the oven.

Finally Jessie got off the phone. "So what do you want for
your birthday?" she yelled from the living room. "Want me to
give you a back massage?"

Jessie got up and walked towards the kitchen. I got on my
knees and opened the oven door. "Check it out," I said. Jessie
crouched down beside me, her elbow leaning against mine, both
of us staring into the oven as if it were a holy shrine demanding
silence and prayer. For a moment I felt a mixture of comfort and
panic, but the panic won out. Or maybe it was the heat in the
kitchen that caused me to jump up, close the oven door, and dash
into the living room.

I showed Jessie more photos I'd taken of friends posing by
the communal gym shower. Fascinated with the steel, space-age
structure, I attempted to demonstrate the contrast between the
human form and modern technology. Underneath the rocket-like
shower, I captured my subjects soaping their bodies, their arms
extended, legs flexed, water swirling over flesh. In one image, the
multiheaded shower appeared to be gushing out rays of sunlight
onto the subjects; in another, the steamy haze made it difficult
to tell where the edges of the imposing steel cylinder ended and
the human body began. Jessie scrutinized a photo of two models
reaching for the shower's control levers. Because I used a slow
shutter speed, the subjects' arms emerged as undulating lines,
"like eels trying to weasel away from their bodies," according to
Jessie.

Since I printed the photos on large sheets of see-through
film, I could manipulate the setting. I highlighted certain sections
of each image with silver paint and used aquamarine paper as a
backdrop. Each rectangular image was now part of a hushed blue
underworld of curves and steel and muscles and mist.

Jessie said, "How the hell did you make these?"

"It's magic," I said.

Jessie cackled. "Guess it is!"

Earlier that day in class, the star photo student, a boy who took crisp black-and-white photos of natural beauty, asked during our photo critique, "What's wrong with a pretty picture?" Sometimes a pretty picture is just what the doctor ordered. But not my doctor. I liked playing, and with some luck I might create a beautiful mess.

A woman from a nearby town saw me taking photos in the gym and assumed I was a stalker. Her husband waited for me outside the locker room. When I pushed the door to leave, he grabbed my camera. "Give me that film!" he said. "You've got pictures of my wife!"

But I held tight to my Pentax. I told him I didn't take pictures of his wife.

Again he grabbed for my camera. "Next thing I know, my wife'll be on the front cover of the newspaper!"

Campus security showed up. They said they'd settle the problem and develop the contact sheet. My friends weren't thrilled with the idea of security guards passing around nude photos of them. Two days later, I picked up the contact sheet. The guards looked at me as if I had smothered a newborn baby and thrown it in a dumpster. Of course the wife was not in the pictures. But by that time, word had gotten out: a student stalker had been taking photos of unsuspecting women in the shower. Everyone heard about my run-in with the law. Even the art department secretary commented, "Oh, you're the one." Yet when my photography teacher saw my work, he accused campus security of infringing on my privacy and freedom of speech and demanded they return my negatives at once. "One of the most imaginative projects I'd ever seen," he wrote in my critique.

Jessie studied the photos of Liz, Belle, and Mandy washing their nude bodies. She looked straight at me. "If you want, I can pose for you too."

"Maybe. If I need more photos," I said, before checking on the carob cake. Jessie picked up the phone and called her boyfriend. My shoulders stiffened. I hid out in the kitchen. Was Jessie trying to come on to me? Did she think I was like *that*? Yet secretly I liked that she liked me. She made me feel desirable, attractive and talented. On the other hand, part of me was repulsed by the idea of Jessie liking me. Later that afternoon, I typed a poem on my Olivetti manual typewriter:

I'm not that way, you're a good friend,
I'm not that way, you're out of luck.
I like you a lot, but the buck
Stops there.

Finally the carob cake baked to perfection. I cut it into rectangles and placed the pieces on two plates, piled high. They looked delicious. I felt proud. I sampled a crumb but couldn't taste the chocolate. All I tasted was bitter dust. Maybe my taste buds weren't working right. I brought a carob rectangle out for Jessie. She hung up the phone, took a bite, and within a few seconds, spit the brownie into the kitchen sink. "What the hell did you put in there?" she screamed, before gagging. "That was the most disgusting thing I've had in my whole life! Tastes like chalk!"

Both of us plopped on the floor and laughed at how delicious the cake looked and how awful it tasted. Obviously we couldn't sell the cake at the co-op. But how could I throw such beautiful works of art in the trash? Might it taste better once it sat for a few hours?

As it turned out, I was supposed to add sugar to unsweetened carob. What if someone liked the taste of unsweetened carob? I left them covered in Saran Wrap on the kitchen counter.

Later that day, Jessie came by and insisted on taking me out for a birthday drink. "You're coming with me. No ifs, ands, or buts. Okay, maybe your butt."

After the first margarita, Jessie tapped my arm while telling me about her lesbian roommate. I yanked my arm away. She ordered us another round. "What do you think of her girlfriend? You like butch women?"

"I never thought about it," I said, feeling a little tipsy. "I have a boyfriend, remember?"

Jessie picked up her tumbler and knocked it against mine. "Here's to our boyfriends," she said. With her eyes focused on the bar's television broadcast of a baseball game, she swigged down half of her drink.

We clanked our glasses together again, this time celebrating my birthday.

"I'm glad you were born," she said, her eyes moving from my face, back to the baseball game.

Jessie insisted we go back to my apartment to meet up with another friend. We stumbled to campus, arm in arm. But on our walk, Jessie asked again if she could pose nude for me. I unlocked my arm from hers. "Are you some kind of exhibitionist?" I asked.

"For you," she said, followed by a cackle.

Thank god we were in front of my apartment. I ran up the stairs and opened the door, and to my amazement, a bunch of friends screamed "Happy Birthday," my first and only surprise birthday party. We ate lasagna and drank tequila shots and Neil Young whined about how you can't be twenty on Sugar Mountain and all the while, unbeknownst to anyone else, guests were sneaking pieces of carob cake in the kitchen. Thinking they weren't supposed to sneak anything, they all suffered in silence. But after everyone was good and drunk, one friend furtively asked another if she tried the cake and the whole roomful of guests concurred: the cake was vile.

Maggie, a friend who gained notoriety for blowing up a campus clothes dryer using a quarter stick of dynamite, decided to take the brownies to the campus pub. "I'll help you get rid of them," she said, giggling. And so out the door she went. Maggie placed the brownies on each end of the bar and watched from the sidelines. Patrons grabbed at them, the bartender taking one for now, one for later. Within seconds, the gagging and spitting and scowling began, and once again campus security was alerted. A guard took a brownie for drug analysis. "It's got to have some kind of drug in it to make it taste so awful," he said.

Although campus security never found out who cooked the brownies, I felt like an outlaw. Two brushes with the law within a week.

I made plans to take more photos of two friends by the communal gym shower. I asked Jessie if she wanted to join them.

She lifted her legs onto the mustard-colored chair in my living room and held her knees. "You really want me to?"

At first she agreed, but five minutes later, she looked out the window. With her back facing me, she asked, "How about I pose for you with my clothes on?"

In my living room, I set up lights and umbrellas and a black velvet backdrop. Jessie, wearing a silk red dress, placed her hands on her hips and puckered her lips. From behind my camera, I focused on her elegant ears, her green eyes, her head-on gaze. Snap. I moved in closer, focusing on her angular profile. Snap.

Suddenly she broke out of her serious stance and laughed. "So, what do you think?" she asked.

I glanced out from behind the camera. "About what?"

Jessie looked out the window. "Do you think I'm sexy?"

I jerked my camera in front of my face and looked through the lens. "You look great in that dress." I could hardly turn the focusing ring on the camera.

Jessie found a comfortable pose, her arms wrapped around her body. But, for a moment, her arms fell to her side and she began to laugh. "Your face is turning beet red!"

As long as the camera stood between us, everything was safe. In one photo, I made sure to capture the cute little birthmark on her chin. And in the final pose, I stood on a chair and captured Jessie's square-jawed, dimpled face looking up at me; for the first time, her green eyes revealed a sadness I hadn't yet seen.

After printing an image of Jessie's profile, I highlighted her ear with silver paint; it looked like a glowing conch shell.

That spring, my boyfriend visited more often. Jessie stayed part-time with her mother. The phone company got wind of the free line.

At the end of the school year, I graduated and moved to New York City with my boyfriend. Jessie graduated a year later and moved to New York City with her junkie boyfriend. Months later, I heard she had broken up with her boyfriend and joined the army.

Seven years after her proposition to pose nude, Jessie phoned me from an army base in Fort Bragg, North Carolina. She had gotten my number from a mutual friend. In the background, her three-month-old baby screamed. She laughed about the kids. "Yeah, one's four and one's new. What a trip being a mother." Her husband, also in the army, was away on active duty. "I was thinking about you," she said, followed by a nervous laugh. Her familiar voice transported me right back to my college apartment, the carob brownies, the tension that I now understood.

I told her about my current job—working as Classified Production Supervisor at the *Village Voice*. How every year since graduation I saved up money and sublet my apartment and traveled Europe for months at a time. And then, out of the blue, she asked if I'd ever been with a woman.

"Yes," I said. "And what about you?"

"Never. But I wanted to. With someone . . ."

"With who?" I asked, already knowing the answer.

"With you. I had a big crush on you, didn't you know that?"

Gratified to hear Jessie acknowledge that tense, scary, exciting feeling, I responded, "I guess I had a crush on you too."

"You guess?" she asked.

"I didn't know it at the time. I just knew I loved hanging out with you."

"This is like having phone sex," Jessie said.

How erotic can a conversation be with a baby screaming in the background?

Eventually she needed to tend to her infant. We promised we'd keep in touch. I wrote her name and address in my phone book with a permanent marker. That year we exchanged Christmas cards.

After I hung up the phone, I could still see Jessie in my college apartment, curled up in a boxy wooden chair with mustard-colored pillows, speaking in hushed tones to her boyfriend. I walk past, smile, and look away, caught up in my own subterranean longing, keeping that mysterious pang at the edge of my heart under wraps.

10

Little Pink Hatchling

At twenty, I had just graduated from college, moved to Manhattan, and got a job selling all-natural Italian ices from a pushcart. Each morning at the Jane Street depot, we packed our carts with blocks of dry ice and big buckets of watermelon, honeydew, cantaloupe, and lemon ices—seeds and all. Our boss, Larry, assigned us a street corner, and if it happened to be in Greenwich Village, we pushed our carts from the depot; if we were assigned a midtown corner, a truck delivered our carts for us. I didn't mind the job. I worked outdoors, got to know different parts of the city, and chatted with people throughout the day. And it gave me a respite from my boyfriend, Joseph, who had moved to New York with me, but a month later moved away, claiming that New York was full of screwed up people and he didn't want to work for "corporate yuppie scum." In particularly bad moods, he'd spit at the ground and say, "I'm going to Avenue C," where drug dealers lined the streets, a death wish for any clean-cut white boy.

We'd been together for a year before moving into a Chinatown sublet along with four of my former classmates. Joseph had been ecstatic to be living in New York. We strolled around fish-smelling streets, ate at Wo Hop on Mott Street, and bought little black bean pies from a Chinese bakery on Mulberry Street. We cooked elaborate meals using fresh bok choy, garlic, scallions, and soy sauce. We sauntered past old synagogues on the Lower East Side, bought sour pickles from barrels near Delancey Street, and walked up to Norfolk Street where, in 1902, my grandmother was born to Jewish immigrant parents from Vilna. On Orchard Street, venders offered us cheap socks and underwear, and across Houston Street on Avenue A, we ate $2.75 chicken dinners at the

Odessa, a Ukrainian diner. Just north of Canal Street, in Little Italy, we split a piece of cheesecake and Joseph spoke of the ongoing battles between his mother's parents from northern Italy and his father's parents from Sicily.

Like our immigrant grandparents and great-grandparents who had come to America via Ellis Island, Joseph and I had discovered a new world of smells, tastes, sounds, and sights. On the streets, we walked arm in arm, our hips snuggled.

When he returned to his parents' home in upstate New York, I had to leave the shared room we rented in the Chinatown loft; I couldn't afford the rent on my own. I moved into an East Village apartment with a friend who also sold Italian ices, a railroad tenement with a bathtub in the kitchen and the pungent smell of death, which I traced to a dead mouse underneath my futon. I got used to the roaches creeping along the walls and by the bathtub, and one day the pipes upstairs burst and a big rat scurried down the piping through our apartment to the apartment below. But I was twenty and glad to be on my own for the first time.

I figured rats and mice and roaches came with the territory, just as Joseph's bad behavior was part of the package. With love and affection came rage. When I showed him my artwork, at first he said, "You're a talented girl." But later in the day, he raged about the frivolity of art and said, "All museums should be destroyed and made into community centers for *The People*." I called him an asshole and ran out of the room. He ran after me, apologized, held me, and said he didn't really mean it.

For a few weeks I was Larry's favorite girl, positioned on the most lucrative corner, Eighth Street and Fifth Avenue, in the heart of Greenwich Village. On a sunny Saturday, the busiest Italian ice day, I pushed my cart to the corner, opened my umbrella, and set up the menu and cups. A minute later, a Colonel Sanders look-alike dressed in white pushed his Good Humor cart close, then rammed it into mine. "This is my corner!" he said. "Find another one!"

"My boss put me here," I said, holding my ground. "I can't leave."

He rammed my cart again. "Get the hell out of here!"

I rammed back and wondered why I couldn't defend myself like this against Joseph. And what he'd think now. He'd probably say something about how the bourgeois college kid was stealing from the working class.

Finally the Good Humor man calmed down. We had a silent standoff. Customers studied our menus.

During a lull, I said, "So how long you been doing this?"

"Thirty years," he said.

"Thirty years?"

"I'm a little retarded," he said.

I sighed. "It's really hot out," I said. "I'm thirsty."

"Did you have lox this morning?" He pulled a bottle of water from his cart. "Want some water?"

I did have lox that morning. "How did you know?"

He poured me a cup of water and handed it to me. "You're thirsty. Drink."

For the rest of the day, in between customers, we talked. He told me about his Chihuahua named Rocket and his brother, a famous economics professor. "You married?" he asked.

"I have a boyfriend," I said.

"Get rid of him," he said.

I scrunched up my face. "Huh?"

"You're too good," he said.

Joseph called and wrote letters, desperately missing me. This was the place where he felt most comfortable, the place where I was just out of reach. He visited for a weekend here and there, and we ate a lot and spent a lot of time in bed. Perhaps this is what I preferred—the idea of Joseph desperately missing me while I went about my day scooping cantaloupe and watermelon and coconut ices. It was easier, safer, less exhausting than dealing with

Joseph in person. During one visit, we played chess, and when it became clear that his king was doomed, he upended the board, punched a hole in my roommate's bedroom door, and stormed out of the apartment. I picked up the pieces.

But Joseph had his charming side, the side that drew me in when we met during my freshman year of college. In round, wire-rimmed glasses and an army jacket, Joseph resembled John Lennon. He'd transferred from a midwestern college, sacrificing a four-year journalism fellowship to get away from a relationship gone bad and to be closer to his high school best friend, Teddy Dover, a chemistry major who lived in the suite down the hall.

"Where are you from?" I asked.

"Liverpool," Joseph said.

"Where are you *really* from?"

"Liverpool, New York," he said, combing his fingers through his thick, brown hair. "A suburb of Syracuse."

Joseph and Teddy considered themselves anarchists and intellectuals. They talked about Karl Marx and Friedrich Nietzsche, and I was convinced they were geniuses. When Joseph asked me a question, I felt nervous, tongue-tied. I uttered short responses that might or might not have related to the question.

Joseph: "So what kind of art do you do?"

Lori: "Pictures of dogs and mirrors. Sometimes doors."

Joseph: "Like the French surrealists?"

Lori: "Miniature poodles too."

Joseph asked me out. I said no. I never had a boyfriend and was scared. So he dated my roommate. And when that didn't work out, he dated another friend. Yet we still hung around together, in the pub, in the cafeteria, on the quad. We played Frisbee for hours at a time. I loved hearing him talk about politics and poetry and the Jersey Pine Barrens, where he had spent his childhood summers.

"Maybe we could take a trip there," he said.

"Yeah, that sounds nice," I said. Our little fantasy.

He called me "Rainy Day," his term of endearment. "You're like a lush, green, rainy forest."

In my junior year, Joseph transferred again, to a college three hours north. But I was still his "Rainy Day." Now and then he sent letters about the political groups he had joined and how we needed to support the Sandinistas in Nicaragua:

> Last night I spray-painted fearsome revolutionary slogans on an evil monument to the state and to militarism at a local park—a huge replica of an air force fighter jet now displays these messages in bright red:
>
> U.S. OUT OF AMERICA
>
> FUCK WAR

He ended his letters with a reference to Jersey: "One of these days . . . wanna go to South Jersey? Or Please don't stray. Surf City is only 200 miles away."

A month before my junior year ended, Joseph visited campus. We sat on my bed and drank White Russians. "These taste like milkshakes," he said, his back against the brick wall.

He moved next to me and put his arm around my shoulder. "You're a goddess."

"Me?"

He took his glasses off. "Yeah, you."

We kissed.

"I thought you were a lesbian," he said.

"Why'd you think that?"

"You wouldn't go out with me at first. And you seemed to really like sparring with women."

"Men wrestle all the time!"

We kissed again.

Joseph invited me to visit him upstate. "The Grateful Dead are playing in three weeks. I'll get tickets."

I got a ride from Acid Sue, who ingested as much acid as

she sold. Once there, Joseph barely greeted me, appearing more interested in entertaining a group of hippie girls. Thank heavens Acid Sue was by my side. At the concert, I wrangled my way up to the front of the stage, away from Joseph, away from his hippie girls who looked at me askance. Afterward, we went back to his friend's house, where hippies in tie-dye sat on dirty couches and talked politics and set up sleeping bags on the floor. I couldn't speak. Too angry, too high on acid, a tape-loop played in my head: *Why did Joseph invite me here? What if I never come down from this acid trip?* At the end of the night, Joseph asked what was wrong. I stared at him, started to bawl, stormed back to the living room, and slipped my body into a sleeping bag.

When the semester ended, I wrote to Joseph: "Why did you invite me to visit and then treat me like a stranger?" He phoned, said he'd gotten involved with another woman and instead of dealing with the situation, had ignored us both. "But I broke up with her," he said. "I only want you." The next day, he came to see me. "I made a terrible mistake," he said, shaking. "Will you come to New Jersey with me? We could go to the boardwalk and see the Pine Barrens."

We checked into a motel by the boardwalk run by an old Ecuadorian couple, and for three nights lounged on crumpled motel sheets and drank port wine and ate cheesecake. We examined each other's bodies, the hidden moles, the little hairs on the back of our necks. We watched *Lifestyles of the Rich and Famous* on TV, ridiculing people whose only concern was money. Joseph said, "I want to devote my life to the struggle of The People." He told me about his anarchist heroes—Sacco and Vanzetti. Holding his body close to mine, I listened intently, not saying much, embarrassed that I didn't have such high-minded aspirations. I just wanted to travel and make art.

As my summer of scooping ices waned, Joseph grew tired of living with his parents in a depressed suburb and working as a school custodian. He wanted to make another go of living in Manhattan, another go of us. I found an East Village apartment and a production job at an Irish-American newspaper. For five months, we cooked gourmet meals, entertained houseguests, worked at respectable jobs. Friends told us that we made a great couple, that we looked alike.

But our stable life lasted only until Joseph lost his paralegal job. He felt proud: "I got fired for using fourteen-letter words." When he fought for unemployment and won, he swelled even more. He was happy to read Kafka all day since he could no longer *be* Kafka. His unemployment ran out but Joseph kept reading. One night when I wouldn't lend him money to buy pot, he sneered at me and muttered, "You're a cheap Jew."

I put my hands on hips and said, "What'd you say?" Now my kibbutz manager's comment about hanging around with "my people" struck a chord.

"Nothing," he said, before taking his death-wish walk on Avenue C. I'm not sure why I let his comments slide. Scraps of love were the norm. And as far as I knew, it was better to be in a relationship than on your own. But what I didn't recognize was that I did fine on my own. What I should have recognized was that I received the opposite of what Aretha Franklin belted out when she sang about "R-E-S-P-E-C-T."

Our conversations revolved around Joseph's refusal to look for a job and the pros and cons of television. I argued that TV made people into idiots; he said The People needed TV after a long day of work on the assembly line. He found a small black-and-white TV in the garbage, jammed a wire hanger in the antenna hole and watched baseball while smoking cigarettes in our living room.

Now Joseph didn't want to escape New York. He wanted to escape me. I told him to leave.

On a sweltering summer morning, Joseph surveyed our tenement flat one last time. "I think I've got everything," he said, eyes

darting around the room. Sweat dribbled down his brow, soaked
through his white undershirt, and clung to his lean, muscular
torso. I wiped the sink and oven with a smelly sponge. Joseph
hoisted the last of his boxes before elbowing the front door open.
"Bye, bye," he said, as if talking to a baby. I fastened the locks,
swept the floor, and smashed a roach dead.

Our relationship was over. For the first time, I'd live alone.
Joseph moved around the corner with his alcoholic buddy and
left me with a roach-infested apartment, an autobiography of
Emma Goldman, and a throng of noisy pigeons outside my
kitchen window.

The pigeons clucked and cooed and rumbled. I yelled for
them to get away, and in seconds wild wing flutter echoed from
the airshaft. Two birds remained. From my refrigerator, I grabbed
a rotten apple and threw it. For a moment I found peace, but
the pigeons returned. "Get the hell out!" I screamed. "This is my
territory!"

It was one of those New York summers when the heat was
too intense for even a snapping turtle, the summer of Cyndi
Lauper's "Girls Just Wanna Have Fun," and I tried my hardest
to do just that. I kissed lots of guys—a tall, skinny Dutchman
who snorted lots of cocaine and worked at the Strand Bookstore, a Jewish writer-guy with a Woody Allen obsession, a
sleazy real-estate investor in oversized aviator glasses who
bought up real estate on the Lower East Side for five thousand
dollars a lot. I went to bars and competed with girlfriends to
see who could get more phone numbers. I met a nerdy computer guy at a party. Two days later he took me out to dinner
and talked really loud—one of those guys who talks so loud
you feel sorry for his date.

In my apartment, I listened to pigeons cooing and making
a racket outside. Again I screamed for them to get away. But
the pigeons wouldn't leave. I threw more rotten apples at them
and added wilted carrots to the ammunition. I listened to bad

Phil Collins songs and cried about Joseph. I missed him. I hated him. I walked by his apartment and tried to run into him. The one time I did, he was sitting on his stoop eating a slice of pizza, grease running down his chin.

"What's up?" he said, his eyes refusing to meet mine.

"I'm on my way to the grocery store," I said.

"I got a job as a law librarian for the Harvard Club," he said, taking a huge bite of pizza.

"You took a job at the *Harvard Club*?"

After he finished chewing, he said, "It pays the rent." He wiped the grease off his face. His hair looked greasy too.

"Call me sometime," I forced out, before running off. I felt paralyzed. How could I let a greasy-faced pseudo-anarchist make me feel this way? Then again, why do so many women put up with unhealthy relationships? Why in our culture is it such a travesty to be alone? Take my friend Susan. Her boyfriend beat her. He heard voices and tried to poke his eyes out with a hanger (he wasn't successful but had red eyes for a while). She said she loved him. She said he was a great lover. Finally he disappeared, only to turn up a month later on an airplane in San Francisco. He tried to hijack the plane using an ax. For a long while, Susan accepted her boyfriend's collect calls from prison.

I needed to leave. The pigeons, the roaches, and most of all, Joseph. I heard about dirt-cheap vacations to Eastern Bloc countries, organized by an eighty-five-year-old British communist from Huddersfield, a coal-mining town in Northern England. I flipped through the folded Xeroxed pages, skimming the descriptions of Polish, Latvian, and Bulgarian trips until I found one to Peking via Budapest and Moscow on the Trans-Siberian Railway. "We could assure you of a splendid holiday at half the usual commercial price." The Trans-Siberian Railway. The trip would depart from England in October. I'd see the Kremlin and Red Square, walk the Great

Wall, travel across Siberia during the dead of winter for the equivalent of six hundred dollars. Since I'd be over there, why not stay awhile and travel through Europe? The dollar was strong, I had money saved, and it wouldn't be a problem to sublet my place.

I booked my ticket but still had two months to go before leaving. I'd see Joseph walking in front of me on Fourteenth Street during the morning rush hour. As the summer wore on, his ass got fatter. Almost bulging out of his pants. *Good*, I thought. *Hope he bloats up into a big wild boar.* Once he stopped off at Disco Donut, a block east of the Union Square Subway Station. I watched him order a glazed donut.

A week later, my phone jerked me awake. I looked at the clock. Midnight.

"Could I come over?" Joseph asked. "I woke up with roaches crawling all over my body."

I took a deep breath. *Fuck him. I should tell him I have company. I should tell him I'm in the middle of a ménage a trois. I should say let the roaches eat you alive, fucking full-of-shit anarchist. Let them eat you and your fat ass too.*

"Hey, it would be great to see you," he said, followed by a sigh. "I miss you."

I hesitated. But I missed him too. "Sure, come over," I said.

We had a history together. We learned to adapt to roaches scurrying across tenement floors, across our bodies, in the middle of the night. We discovered sticky roach traps and took pleasure in checking on the catch of the day, those writhing hieroglyphics in all shapes and sizes, wiggling their torsos until they didn't.

Our reunion lasted for the evening. At least in China I wouldn't have to run into Joseph.

The daily pigeon routine took on a new twist. A neatly arranged circle of twigs appeared on my bathroom ledge. I swept them away. *No you don't, you fuckers! Not on my ledge!*

When the circle of twigs reappeared, I brushed them away again. *Why the hell did I let that asshole stay over?*

The next time I checked my ledge, three speckled eggs lay in the nest's center. I would have to be a monster to sweep them away.

Three little pink hatchlings with eyes filling their faces replaced the eggs. A plump, rumbling mother pigeon glowered at me. This annoying, filthy mother-bird started out just as sweet. I wanted to run to the nearby bodega and buy a Cuban cigar.

Each day, I checked on the pigeons. I left them scraps of stale bread. I even named the babies: Eduardo, Maria, and Cecelia. Now they were my family. I didn't need a fat-assed, greasy-faced anarchist.

The day before I took off on my European adventure, I checked on the baby pigeons. But they had already flown from the darkened airshaft into sapphire blue skies. A thick-woven nest remained, its hardened layers built up from a loose circle of twigs. I slid the nest off the ledge and within seconds heard a satisfying thump echo back.

11

Slow Train to the Forbidden City

I press Play. On the television screen, Rita cocks her head and squints, a suspicious look on her face. She still looks like the woman I had met over twenty years ago on a month-long British Communist package tour to Russia and China via the Trans-Siberian Railway, when both of us were in our early twenties. But now heavy creases line her eyes. She brushes strands of long blonde hair from her face and grins an impish smile when our eyes meet.

In a desperate attempt at getting answers, I had come up with the idea of filming an interview with Rita; in all the time I'd known her, our conversations had been stilted, cryptic. Maybe a camera would act as a pair of safety goggles or better yet, X-Ray Specs, magical glasses through which the wearer could see bones through hands. But instead of bones, I wanted to see the truth.

In college, expressing myself through art helped me make sense of my life, but in New York, between lack of money and access to equipment and time, I didn't do much photography. When I traveled for long periods, starting on the Trans-Siberian Railway, I started to journal, to write poetry, to play with language. I no longer had access to a darkroom, I no longer had my bag of tricks, but I had words. And my collection of words led me to a master's program in creative writing, which led me to the teaching of writing, which led me to a doctorate in English, which led me to a full-time job as a college professor.

Since I had a teaching gig in Cambridge, England, why not take a side trip and interview Rita?

On camera, Rita says, "What are you going to ask me?"

"About your life," I say. My heart is thumping, my brow sweating, but I shove forward. We're in her living room, on an orange ragged sofa facing a wall cluttered high with books, somewhere in the countryside, an hour from London. Behind me, through the windows, is a large yard, a laundry line saddled with jeans and shirts. Now that I've gathered the confidence, the voice to really talk, it's now or never. Rita, this settled, middle-aged "wifey," had once thrown me into a world of new ideas and feelings. She was the first woman I fell for. Knee deep and head on. In her presence, my heart opened—and shattered. And as far as I could tell, she skipped away into the sunset, never to acknowledge the strewn pieces left behind.

I ask Rita to state her name and occupation. She speaks about her work for educational charities using video as a group development tool. She's been doing this for years, receiving local, national, and international grants to help, for example, Israelis and Palestinians make sense of each other. But now I've got the camera. Now I'm using it as an educational tool.

She clasps her hands and looks at me as if she knows what I'm after. I sit up straight, poke my face out, and stare hard to make sure she knows I mean business. After a long pause, I ask her what she remembers about the Trans-Siberian trip.

She talks about finding herself in front of the tour bus at London's King's Cross Station with a microphone in her hand— she led the trip. "Talking and drinking with people in carriages," she says. "I actually don't remember a lot. I didn't have a camera. I was going through a phase where I didn't want to experience life through a lens."

"You did have a camera," I say. "You let me use it when mine broke."

The tour bus had taken our group to Budapest, where we boarded a big green train that would carry us over eight time zones. I shared my compartment with three women: Mary, who only drank Spirulina and was on the run from her fiancé; Marjorie, who wore earrings of bone and embezzled money from a bookstore until it went out of business; and blonde-haired, blue-eyed Rita, who had taught English in China for two years and, since she spoke Chinese, had been hired to be courier for the trip.

From the first day, Rita, always a bit disheveled-looking in a wrinkled shirt and black leggings, stood near me. We watched rivers and mountains and towns whoosh by. We talked about men, politics, and our love of travel. On the second day of the trip, Rita spoke about Simone de Beauvoir, a French feminist, and de Beauvoir's lifelong relationship with philosopher Jean-Paul Sarte. "But they never lived together," Rita said, "and they both had other lovers."

"Sounds complicated," I said. Cleavage spilled from her tight burgundy sweater. I steered my eyes to the floor.

"It's the ideal situation," she said, before going off on the institution of marriage. "It's so bloody ridiculous. Imagine sleeping with the same person every night for the rest of your life. How boring!" She gripped the railing by the window until I could see the whites underneath her fingernails.

I never thought marriage was such a bad idea, but maybe Rita had a point.

I told her about Joseph, his supposed left-wing, anarchist ideals. "But when it came to cleaning the apartment," I said, "he refused to lift a finger until he saw cockroaches multiplying."

"Bloody men," Rita said, rolling her eyes.

Joseph, for all of his talk, did nothing to actually help "The

People," unlike Rita, who produced educational videos, organized rallies and benefits, and put together a monthly magazine, *Rise Up.*

On the third day of the trip, Rita invited me to explore the train with her. "Don't you want to practice your Russian?" she asked, fingers combing through her hair.

My knowledge of Russian was limited to basic greetings and single digit numbers, but yes, I wanted to explore with Rita. Still in her black leggings, she now wore a tight-fitting T-shirt with the words "Anger, Use It!" We walked up and down the train's corridors—passageways reeking of coal, garlic, and foul cigarettes, a smell I grew fond of. Eastern Bloc passengers brought all the amenities they needed: greasy fish, babka bread, cabbage. Some had live chickens *buck-buck-bucking.* I smiled at a hearty old Russian woman and in return, she invited us into her cabin for fish and cakes. After eating more than I should have—I pantomimed a full stomach—the woman screamed, "*Nyet, Nyet!*" and shoved more food towards me. I gave her a pack of Wrigley's gum and a new pair of pantyhose, two items I had stocked up on beforehand to give as gifts, both inaccessible in Eastern Bloc countries, and, as if she'd won the lottery, the Russian woman smiled bright and radiant, clutching the yellow pack of gum, fingering the "One Size Fits All" sticker on the hosiery box.

Once the train chugged onto Russian soil, Rita mentioned she had a large amount of Russian currency on her. The organizer of the trip had given her the money to pay for the group's accommodations. Yet it was illegal to have so much money without a record of exchange. Reason enough for imprisonment. Before the border police came aboard, I volunteered to hold the money in my sock, under my heel. When the coast was clear, I handed the sweaty bills back to Rita, high off the rush of not getting caught.

By the fourth day, when Rita wasn't by my side, I longed for her. What the hell was going on with me? I couldn't be a lesbian, could I? Wouldn't I already have figured that out? After all, I went to a college where the largest organization on campus was the gay and lesbian union. Unlike the handful of lesbians I knew, I didn't have spiky blue hair or look like a nun. I was a shy Jewish girl from Long Island with long frizzy hair that I spent hours on end trying to blow-dry straight.

I'm not like that. Don't let me be like that! And the train moseyed on.

Every four or five hours, the train picked up passengers along the way. Rita and I had fifteen minutes to run onto the platform and buy cookies and dumplings and cans of sardines and Lenin pins. All the while, I couldn't make eye contact with her without blushing and I waited for this sentiment to pass, but it pulled up alongside me and stared me in the face.

The Russian countryside, turning and twisting, wrapped around rivers, mountains, and cornfields. The rhythm of the train clacked upon tracks and steeped, like black Russian tea, into my blood. It became my lifeline. This was my world: warmth, motion, tea from a samovar for the equivalent of two cents, a growing fixation on Rita, and the sun, rising and falling.

Heat blasted from the train's vents, but the windows were screwed shut. The official word on this—the Soviet government ordered the windows locked so foreigners couldn't escape into Russia. I got used to the heat and walked around in a tank top in the middle of the Siberian winter.

A teenage boy wearing a turquoise sweatsuit stared at my two-dollar LCD watch and offered me ten rubles (about fifteen dollars). I followed him into his cabin and he stuffed the ruble wad in my hand. Again I felt a thrill off of getting away with something, of beating the system. When a big bearded Freud-looking man caught me in between train cars and in a low gravelly voice asked, "Do you have *Playboy*?" I sold him my sneakers. From that point on, I had to wear my fashionable army boots. A retired health inspector, a member of our group, commented, "A woman shouldn't be wearing army boots."

"I quite like them," Rita responded.

Chugging deeper into Siberia, land of forced labor camps, I couldn't stop thinking about Rita, the way she caressed her hair, the way she said, "I can't be bothered" when speaking about a high-paying career.

Every so often, Charles, a twenty-eight-year-old Maoist with awful body odor, would politely ask if he could join our conversations. By the way he glanced at Rita, he clearly was smitten as well. He tried to impress her by talking about quantum relativity and quoting from Mao's *Little Red Book*. Rita complained about his smell, but I could tell she liked the attention.

One night Charles sat across from us, focused on me, then her, then me, then his watch, then her, then me, then his watch, and asked, "Are you two having a lesbian affair?"

"What's it to you if we were?" Rita said.

I giggled and stared at my shoes, felt my face turn red and my shoulders hunch. How the hell did he know what was going on? Did he think I *looked* like a lesbian? Nothing was going on! Not in any physical way, apart from my supposed fascination with her feet. She had odd bunions, and all I could do was inspect them every so often and offer foot massages. I kneaded her tender heels, rubbed her supple ankles, gently pulled at her luscious toes, examined her curious arches that neatly slipped into a pair of Chinese slippers. I even had her pose her feet for my camera.

Despite the icy platforms and freezing of the inside of my nose, I continued to step off the train during our fifteen-minute stops. Russian women in babushkas sold cakes wrapped in *Pravda* pages. Dense-as-blackbread women tapped ice off the train wheels with iron batons. On a Siberian train platform, Rita took a picture of me holding up chewing gum packets and pantyhose. "How cute," she said. "The American Capitalist in Siberia."

The next day, Ronald Reagan, who called the Soviet Union an evil empire, was re-elected. Joseph and I had marched in the streets of Manhattan that summer, demanding the United States stop funding the Contras, U.S.-supported mercenaries fighting against the Soviet-supported Nicaraguan government, the same summer the Soviet Union boycotted the Olympics in Los Angeles.

Every so often Russian guards rummaged through our belongings, searching for anti-Russian propaganda. They asked us to gather our printed matter—books, magazines, journals—and then they'd flip through the pages. They confiscated *Newsweek*, *The Herald Tribune*, and a roll of film. Jimmy, a seventy-five-year-old Scotsman who dressed in a kilt and played his bagpipes at every stop along the way, didn't understand why the guards confiscated his film. "They asked me if I had taken pictures of railway stations," he said. "I told them I took pictures of a gorgeous sunset from the train window, when we stopped at a station."

One night a guard flipped through a journal of my simplistic cartoon-like drawings. He focused on one particular picture titled "Super Mosquito." I had drawn a mosquito flexing its muscles, with a big Superman *S* on its torso. He looked at me, his brow furrowed, asked, "What is this? Explain?"

Rita, lying on the couchette above mine, watched from above.

"It's just a mosquito," I said. To demonstrate, I poked my arm with my index finger. "*Buzz buzz*. It's an insect."

The guard studied the drawing again, then looked up. "What does it mean?"

"It means nothing," I said. "It's humor. You know, ha ha."

What else could I say about a stupid drawing? Ten minutes later, two female interpreters stepped into the cabin and asked me what the drawing meant.

"It's just a mosquito," I said. "It means nothing. It's supposed to be funny."

They asked to see my passport, studied my photo, my name.

"You are American?" one of the interpreters asked.

The three Russians conferred. The male guard motioned for me to rip the drawing up. And I did.

An hour later, I drew another "Super Mosquito." I showed the new drawing to Rita. "What do you think?"

"Those Russians," she said, "can be so bloody paranoid." Two days later, when a new set of Russian police came aboard to check our printed matter, I hid the journal at the bottom of my backpack.

Rita taught me the Chinese greeting meaning, "Hello, have you eaten yet?" She tried to teach me Tai Chi, but my ability to focus was impaired. One night I massaged her head. My fingers ran across her skull, through her thick mane and back to her temples. At one point she caught me looking at her, shut her eyes, and smiled.

Once we arrived in Peking, our Chinese guide met us with a megaphone in hand to accompany us to a hotel where we washed our filthy bodies and socks. I leaned out the bus window and heard a rhapsody of clanking bike bells. In this land of jade and dragons and gongs, a carnival of rushing rickshaws and people and more people in blue and green Mao suits flashed by. Everywhere our group went, Chinese people stared at us. They lined up, stood with open mouths and wide eyes. And we too lined up, to see Mao's dead body, his jaundiced corpse preserved under glass.

Our group followed the megaphone, and all roads led to tourist shops where we used special tourist money. After the shopping mall/bomb shelter tour, a Chinese woman stood in front of me, frozen. I broke her stance with the "Hello, have you eaten yet?" greeting. She came to life and rambled on about what, I'll never know.

While the rest of the group went to the Peking Circus, Rita and I drank beer in her hotel room. She let me see her new acupuncture kit. "You could practice on me," I said. Rita showed me the meridian points on my hands and arms. When she touched me, goosebumps rose. I pointed to the 1960s style TV set in the room. "Think there's anything good on TV?" I asked.

"Not unless you want to watch the same propaganda over and over," Rita said, "about happy farmers in the countryside."

Rita found more meridian points. For a moment, we locked eyes. I asked her how long she'd been with her ex-boyfriend.

"Two years," she said. "And you?"

"Too long," I said.

Rita packed up her acupuncture kit. "Let's go get a drink downstairs."

The next day we walked along the Great Wall, away from tourists, to where it was rundown and we stopped and stared at the miles of mountains and jagged branches and endless wall. We sat silent upon one of the only man-made sites decipherable from the moon, or at least that was what I'd heard.

"Think about it," Rita said. "All the labor, blood, and sweat that helped build this wall."

I tried to imagine the half-starved work crews, the mortar and brick, but I couldn't picture anything but Rita, holding her, kissing her.

We talked about our futures. "I want to make art," I said.

"If you believe in what you do," she said, combing her fingers through her hair, "the rest will follow."

Rita told me about her dream of fighting racism and empowering women through her video work.

Later that day, our group observed a roomful of mostly schoolboys sing about hoeing and tranquility; I couldn't help but feel the ghosts of aborted girls. In Peking's Forbidden City, all the information about jade and war and gold couldn't grab my attention the way Rita did.

After the China trip, I traveled another month in Europe. I climbed the Eiffel Tower and bought salami in East Berlin. I drank a hundred cups of espresso and watched old men hobble along cobblestone roads, young couples embrace, tourists study Foder's guides. Everyday I thought I saw Rita walking by, on the

metro, in the theatre, in the Dusseldorf Burger King. Every train
door slammed out Rita's name. My world was flooded by hole-
punched train tickets, sounds of teacups and saucers and little
spoons, and light beams of possibility.

Three days before flying back to New York, I found myself a
little tipsy (after drinking multiple pints of lager at a local pub),
lying on Rita's bed in London, both of us staring at the ceiling.
We listened to Kraftwerk's *Trans-Europe Express*. I told her about
Joseph, how I had heard through friends he missed me and
loved me and felt terrible. He called friends and family to get my
address. I didn't have one. He wrote love letters and sent them to
Crete, on the off chance I might have stayed at the youth hostel I
stayed at three years before.

"What will you do?" Rita asked.

"If I get back together with him," I said, staring at the ceiling,
"I'll tell him I want to see other people too."

Before I could think about what I was doing, I moved my
body next to hers and wrapped my arm around her waist. She
turned towards me and held me. We kissed. Kraftwerk's album
played over and over and over again, our arms and legs and
sweat intertwined, our hands moving, gliding up and down each
other's bodies, and finally, finally I felt at ease, in a foreign land.
For hours, but not long enough, we kissed and touched, until the
door bell rang and Rita jumped up and ran to greet Martin—her
lanky, hunched-shouldered ex-lover and video business partner.
The three of us went for dinner, Rita and I flushed in the cheeks.

For three days, we learned each other's curves and smells
and blemishes. So this was love, I thought, an undying love
with a woman. And though I did get back together with
Joseph after I returned to New York, I began to live out Rita's
philosophies. I dated men and women, all the while waiting
for Rita's sporadic letters, usually filled with updates about her
political work and her video business with Martin and always,

just before the end of the letter, she threw me a crumb: *I miss you* or *I can't wait to see you again!* Enough for me to swoon. Meanwhile, no one could mess with me because I was a hipster bisexual artsy chick who had it all.

Nine months after I left Rita, she phoned me. She invited me on a ten-day holiday to Romania via the Orient Express. "I'm the courier," she said. "No one will notice if you 'crash.' We'll stay in a first-class hotel on the Black Sea, all meals and transportation included. All you pay for are the visas." She reminded me that the tour company, known for its massive disorganization, would work in our favor. In fact, rumor had it that on one of the tour company's earlier trips to Leningrad, an old woman died on the train. "Instead of dealing with Russian bureaucracy," Rita said, "before the passport guards came around, the tour organizer propped her up, passport in hand. The ruse worked."

"Sounds great!" I said. Crashing a trip should be easier than getting through passport control with a dead woman. I sublet my apartment, emptied my savings account, quit my newspaper production job, and flew to England.

At the train station in London, Rita hugged me and led me into her car. "So good to see you," she said. We held hands for a minute before she pulled hers away to shift gears. At her house, Martin got up from the kitchen table. "We're going to have a blast on the trip!" he said, his Romanesque nose wriggling up and down before he blew it into a filthy handkerchief.

I let my backpack thump to the floor. A big ant scurried by. I stomped on it. "You're going too?"

Rita twirled a strand of her disheveled mane, licked her lips, offered me tea. "We'll have a brilliant time together!"

I swallowed hard. I wanted to yell, *I thought it was just you and me and a busload of communists!* But instead, I picked up a fork and poked it lightly into my hand.

Setting my tea down, Rita said, "I figured you and Martin could pretend to be a couple, so people don't suspect that you're both crashing." She lifted her shirt up just a little and rubbed her belly.

Rita led me to her bedroom. "I'll be right back," she said. "Martin and I have to mail this grant proposal in. Make yourself comfortable."

On her dirty, piss-colored loveseat, I tried to rest my eyes, breathe, stay calm. I told myself not to be paranoid about Martin coming along; they were good friends. We'd have a good time together. I tried to read a Xeroxed magazine I picked up from the floor, a fist on the cover and the words "Smash the System" underneath. After a long flight, after months of obsessing about Rita, the last place I wanted to be was alone in that dark bedroom littered with dirty teacups, especially the one with a layer of mold on top. After fifteen minutes of waiting, I swooped up a letter with a thick-penned heart and arrow lying on the floor amidst the cups and saucers. "Hey girl . . . had an amazing time with you and can't wait to see you again. Until the next time, John."

When Rita barreled through the door, the letter was still in my hand. "How are you?" she asked.

We watched the letter drift downwards.

She plopped herself next to me, leaned her head against my shoulder. "It's so good to see you," she said, tossing her head back. And despite Martin, despite the letter, I fell right into Rita's curves.

On the Orient Express, Rita, Martin, and I settled into a three-person berth. We lined up our alcohol and began to chug beer and brandy in celebration of my twenty-fourth birthday. When I was good and drunk and parched, I left the berth to search for bottled water, and upon my return, found Rita and Martin making out. I picked up my camera and threatened to take a picture. But if the moment were captured on film, it surely would have become real.

Martin left the berth. I poured myself a shot of brandy and looked out the window but all I saw was my bitter reflection.

"You okay?" Rita asked.

I kept looking at my reflection.

She patted the cushion next to her. "Come here," she said.

I moved next to her and stared at my shoes. "Who are you with?" I asked. "Martin or me?"

She leaned over to kiss me. "I'm with you!"

"So we'll share a hotel room together?"

She moved in to embrace me. "Of course."

Martin slid the door open and Rita jumped up. Behind him, a smeared-lipstick Romanian stumbled into our berth. "My name Katrina," she slurred out. "I speak little English." She flopped her body onto a seat and handed me a picture of her son. "Him beautiful. Yes?" She told us her husband had been arrested and received a two-year jail sentence.

"What for?" I asked.

She looked out the window, a grim expression on her face, lit a cigarette. "America, good?"

The next morning, passengers smoked rancid cigarettes in the aisles while the train chugged across the Transylvanian mountains. Rita and Martin sat side by side, listening to the same Walkman. I stared out the window, hungover, drinking sickly sweet orange soda. Hundreds of black particles floated at the bottle's bottom.

Martin had to share a room with an old deaf man for the entire trip. In the dining hall, he puffed his cheeks, tapped his fingers on the table. Dour-faced hotel workers threw tiny plates of wilted lettuce in front of us, each dressed with a blob of crusty mayonnaise.

Rita touched Martin's arm, a concerned expression on her face. "I'm so sorry," she said.

None of us ate the food, but we drank plenty of cheap Romanian wine, which kept us good and drunk.

On state television, I watched Nicolae Ceausescu, the president of Romania, entering well-stocked stores, crowds of people cheering behind him. What I didn't know: he executed poets and outlawed typewriters and exported the country's food while his own people starved. To boost the population, he put an end to abortion and contraception. Every woman forty-five and under had to produce a minimum of five children. He pitted one ethnic group against another, making it hard for groups to band together against him. He recruited schoolchildren to spy on friends, parents, and teachers. I had no clue about Ceausescu's military dictatorship or the reasoning behind overcrowded Romanian orphanages. I agreed to go to Romania for one reason—to be with Rita.

The three of us spent hours on the beach, Rita staring at Martin, me staring at Rita, wondering why she invited me. Was this my punishment for getting involved with a woman in the first place?

On the second day, out on the scorching beach, Martin bellowed into his harmonica. He was terrible. "That sounds really good," Rita said.

During meals, an Oxford University student on the trip, a Paul McCartney look-alike, sidled up to Rita and recited lines from Sylvia Plath and William Blake. As far as he knew Martin and I were together, and Rita was up for grabs.

One afternoon, I caught a chambermaid rummaging through my luggage. When she saw me, she started to fold my clothes. Missing from my bag—a cheap pair of sunglasses and two ballpoint pens. It was easier to climb the nine flights of stairs to our room than confront the glaring women who worked the hotel elevators, the same women who offered to change money in the bathroom.

On the fifth day of the trip, Rita asked if she could spend the day with Martin. "I need to talk things out with him," she said.

I walked three miles to the nearby city of Constanza, where Roman poet Ovid was exiled in 8 AD for reasons not fully known, but Ovid himself described his offenses as a "poem"—perhaps, some speculate, *The Art of Love*. There, I took in a photography exhibit of blurry babies, the pictures hanging lopsided on moldy walls. On the way back, I passed a shop window displaying a naked doll surrounded by cigarette lighters and Bic pens. Outside, a legless man pointed to his scale. For about three cents, I could learn my weight. All I wanted was a nap.

But when I walked towards my room, along with Rita's familiar moans, bedsprings squealed through the door. I knocked and heard more bedsprings. I banged again, this time with gusto.

"Just a minute," Rita yelled.

I stormed off to the bar, drank one brandy after the next.

We still had four days to go. At the time, it took months to reserve train tickets in Eastern Europe.

When I met Rita on the boardwalk later that day, I threw my arms up. "So you got what you wanted!" I said.

Rita played with her hair, exposing her hairy armpit. "This doesn't affect the way I feel about you."

"It affects the way I feel about you!" I snapped. Two soldiers strolled by. One smiled, exposing a black front tooth. The sun began to descend. "Would you have invited Martin," I asked, "if I were a guy?"

With arms by her side, she looked down. "I never meant for this to happen," she said.

I knew one woman on the trip, a depressed philosophy professor, who didn't have a roommate. I was certain that if I explained the situation, she'd let me room with her. "For your information," I said, "I'll be rooming with the clinically depressed philosophy professor. Starting tonight!"

Rita stared at me with her mouth half open. "You don't need to do that."

"Why didn't you tell me," I said, "that you were going to invite your boyfriend?"

"He's not my boyfriend," she said.

"Did he know what was going on between us?"

Rita moved a strand of hair from her eyes. "I suppose not." She stepped forward and hugged me. "Honestly. I didn't mean for this to happen."

Later that night, on the same bed where she had just screwed Martin, she reached out to caress my arm. I curled up next to her and held her, moved my body on top of hers and kissed her, first gently, then aggressively. With fingers and tongues and arms, we swallowed one another, until our bodies were covered in sweat, until the bed shifted a few inches to the left, until we groaned and shuddered into nothing but silence and the deafening ticks of Rita's alarm clock.

We took a bus from the hotel to Constanza, just the two of us, so she could buy a birthday present for Martin. Still, we didn't talk about our situation. Rather, we gossiped about the tour-group members, focusing on a little white-haired man, a Stalinist, who praised the Romanian government for providing everyone with work and access to health care.

"How bloody stupid he is," Rita said. "Doesn't he see that everyone in this country is completely miserable?"

Good observation, I should have said.

That evening our tour group sat on ornate couches, just outside the dining hall, waiting for dinner to be served. Martin plucked at his new mandolin—Rita's present. When the Oxford Boy asked Martin where he had gotten the instrument, he pointed to me, his supposed girlfriend. "Lori gave it to me. For my birthday."

Rita had given me a set of black-and-white postcards of a women's peace encampment for my birthday. I would have preferred a mandolin.

For the remainder of the trip Martin kept his distance, but
Rita made sure to spend "alone time" with him before coming
back to our room at night. I waited in the hotel room, envisioning
spy cameras lodged in the dropped ceiling, Romanian officials
observing the drama between two young Western women and an
unwitting male cohort.

On the hotel's thirteenth floor, Rita and I went to a disco.
Outside the disco, on the balcony, we kissed. An obese man on
the other side of the balcony stared at us. He wouldn't stop looking. At least we had a witness.

On the train back, at one point Martin and I were alone in
the berth. I didn't resent him. Like me, he hadn't known what he
was getting himself into.

"So how long do you think it'll take to recover from our jour-
ney?" I asked.

"Five years," Martin said, his head swaying from side to side.

"Ten," I said.

We agreed on twenty.

I'd like to say I never saw Rita again. I'd like to say I got up in
her face and told her how selfish she was for disrespecting me,
and for that matter, for demeaning all women who like women.
But I didn't. Instead, over the next year we continued to see each
other. She visited me in New York. We never mentioned Martin.
We never mentioned what had gone on between us. Our story
was still off-limits to even us. We lived our secret. A stupid secret
that became part of me, a land mine sitting at the bottom of my
heart, evidence this was all I deserved.

Now, more than twenty years later, I ask Rita what she remembers
about Romania.

"The interrogation has finally arrived," she says. She shifts in her seat, rubs her temple. "It was a little naïve of me to invite both you and Martin."

I ask if she's uncomfortable.

Rita purses her lips, says, "This dynamic with you having the camera is a bit defensive-making."

Without the camera, the interview wouldn't take place. The camera was a witness. I needed a witness, like that fat Romanian man.

"Why do you think," I said, "we never talked about what was going on?"

"I wasn't brought up to talk," Rita says, "As a teenager I went through a period when I was depressed and anorexic. My mom used to say, 'For goodness sakes! Put a smile on your face.' We British don't talk."

I spoke about my internalized homophobia, of living in a world where the word *lesbian* was dangerous, dirty, and wrong.

Rita, a serious expression on her face, nods her head.

"It took me years," I say, "to accept myself, to accept my sexuality." What I don't tell Rita—it had been a painful process. And being dissed in Romania by my first female lover had confirmed that loving another woman would inevitably lead to a painful and clandestine life.

"If you could go back in time," I say, "what would you have asked me?"

She strokes her hair. "What are you feeling? Where is it going? Anywhere? What did it mean for you?" And then Rita looks at me. "What *did it* mean for you?"

"You flicked a switch that let me see the world in a completely different light," I say.

Rita stares at me, says, "You arrived and I fell into this deep feeling and then you were gone. It was quite confusing." She crosses her legs and continues. "I wanted to maintain contact. But I felt a lot of guilt. Maybe it's about me not giving enough time to my emotional life. I'd rather be planning," she says, "than reflecting."

We switched places. Now Rita videotaped me. Without the camera, I'm exposed. Raw. My terrified face fills the television screen. Rita asks about Romania.

I take a deep breath. "I was devastated."

Rita asks if I'm okay.

I wave to the camera. Fake smile.

"I knew you were hurt," she says, "but I didn't feel in control. I came to visit you in New York after Romania, didn't I? It doesn't make sense."

"When you came to New York," I say, "I thought I was a rock star. I had two boyfriends and two girlfriends and thought I had it all. I was an idiot."

During Rita's stay, she spent a good part of her days visiting anarchist contacts living in the Grand Street co-ops. She'd leave early in the morning and, once again, left me alone. Thank heavens Joseph comforted me. Together we poked fun at Rita's behavior, how the feminist mantra "The personal is political" didn't quite mesh with her actions.

"I was an idiot too," Rita says. "I was writing things about how fantastic non-monogamy was. At the time I genuinely believed in what I was writing and doing. Not until I got hurt and hurt lots of people did I change views."

I stare into the camera, a scared, relieved look on my face. I'm getting what I wanted: an explanation, an apology. An understanding of how I was a key player.

Rita talks even more when the camera is pointed at me. "When I felt something emotionally," she says, "I shut down. I always coped with life by shutting down. I still do."

Before setting out for Rita's house earlier in the day, I had spent time with Marjorie, the embezzler I met on the Trans-Siberian trip. I told her about my plans to videotape Rita. Marjorie advised me against it. "Let it go," she said. "You can't live in the past. Move on." I told her I needed to do this; I had no choice. "This is my story," I said. "I deserve to know what happened."

Later that evening, I showed the videotape to Marjorie. "That was fascinating," she said. "Rita's really grown up."

Rita and I strolled through a field behind her house. She told me it hadn't been an easy road since Romania. She had two miscarriages. She mentioned again how easy it was to shut down. "Sex was the simple part," she said.

We stopped walking and hugged each other.

Despite her earlier revolutionary ideals, she was now living a mainstream life with husband and child. I was the out lesbian, the nomad moving from one relationship to the next, still searching for a family. Yet inside Rita's house, there was a dank, heavy feel, like an old museum with relics that needed a good dusting.

Rita mentioned her new vacation home in Bulgaria, near the Black Sea. "You should come visit," she said, before looking at me with a half grin. "But maybe you don't want to do another Black Sea holiday with us."

I touched the little birthmark on her chin. "Maybe not," I said.

Martin returned from a camping trip he'd taken with their six-year-old son, Roger. Martin's hair was gray, his back hunched, his eyes wrinkled, yet he was still attractive in his own way. He greeted me with a warm embrace. Even in this time warp, I felt a certain comfort in the room. I knew these faces, voices, gestures.

Roger hid behind Martin's leg, one of his eyes peering out.

Rita said to Roger, "Say hello to Lori. She's come all the way from America to see us."

He smiled and held up his G.I. Joe doll.

"Hello Roger," I said.

I pointed the camera at Martin and Roger.

On the television screen, Martin waves. Roger waves too. "Hello, America," Martin says.

"Hello, America," Roger repeats.

I panned the camera up to Rita's face. "Hello, America," she says.

The video ends. The screen turns blue.

12

New York: 1986–89

It's 1989 and Paula calls from San Francisco to tell me that Barry, her ex-boyfriend, tested positive for AIDS. "What if I have it too?" she asks.

I try to comfort her. I tell her she probably doesn't have it, that it's been two years since she's been with Barry. But I worry about her. Out my sixth-floor East Village tenement window, the Twin Towers loom in the distance, white church steeples in the forefront. I tell Paula about Pete, a typesetter I had worked with who died of AIDS. "He shot up all the time. No one had a clue. We just thought he was a drunk."

"Who would have thought sex could be so deadly?" Paula asks. Back in college she said variety was the spice of life, that's why she slept with so many men. And the worst consequence of her actions was a minor case of crabs.

Now she says she'll get her test results in two days. I wish her luck and hang up the phone.

And meditate about a time when I held fast to Paula's "variety is the spice of life" motto, when at twenty-four I was fearless, a rock star, too good for monogamy, too cool for commitment. I had two boyfriends and a girlfriend and Rita, who had plans to visit.

A time when heroin and crack dealers hung out in front of my East Village apartment, an area where art galleries popped up on every corner, an area bought up by real estate moguls who jacked up rents so only wealthy foreigners and stockbrokers could afford to live there, a time when Donald Trump let prostitutes and drug dealers live rent-free in his buildings under the guise of helping the homeless, when all the while he was trying to scare off tenants who lived in affordable apartments. A time when my boyfriend Joseph, who I'd been with since I was nineteen, on and off but mostly on, agreed to open up our relationship, to date other people. So I called a handsome-in-that-Hugh-Grant-kind-of-way Brit I had met at Bowl-Mor Lanes on University Place in the heart of Greenwich Village, where every Saturday night a group of friends bowled to the sounds of Motown and rock 'n roll. The Brit was just out of a relationship with a heroin addict, had his own carpentry business, his own studio apartment, and his own vehicle, a retired postal jeep. Besides that, he had gone to boarding school with Prince Andrew in Scotland, and for sure this would be the closest to royalty I would ever come.

I asked the Brit over for dinner and he accepted. I prepared chicken, seared and sautéed in tomato sauce, uncorked a bottle of Romanian wine, took note of his big white teeth and pale blue eyes, and made sure to keep refilling our cups. We played footsy and talked and laughed, and I thought *Thank god for alcohol*, which gave me the confidence to lead the Brit to my futon on the floor, where we fumbled and groped, and it was gentle and tender, and I wasn't worried about catching deadly diseases from him via his ex-girlfriend the junkie.

After all, bathhouses for gay men were still profitable businesses and HIV was not yet part of our vocabulary, so why worry about death when we could dance to the techno sounds of Frankie Goes to Hollywood, The Human League, and Jimmy Somerville's cover of Donna Summer's "I Feel Love"?

In the morning, the Brit and I ate breakfast at the Kiev, a Ukrainian diner owned by Indians who employed buxom blonde Polish waitresses, waitresses who served kielbasa and

eggs and blintzes, waitresses who all the artsy guys in the East
Village were in love with.

The Brit laughed at my jokes, called often, and bought me
presents from street vendors on Astor Place, including a black
and yellow polka-dotted vest, a book on medieval philosophy,
and an old Brownie camera. It was common knowledge that most
of the merchandise sold on the street had been stolen from cars
and apartments or found in the trash, and one day, when I saw a
vendor selling a vacuum cleaner and freshly cut slabs of red meat
on the sidewalk, I tried not to think too hard about where the
meat came from.

The Brit didn't know about Joseph, but Joseph knew about
the Brit, and when he met the Brit through a mutual friend, he
later commented about how I was going out with fancy people,
people too fancy for the likes of him. Joseph, whose idea of fun
was getting drunk and throwing rocks at seagulls, reading exis-
tential literature, and eating corned beef hash at the local diner,
grew up in a working-class family in upstate New York, far from
European princes and kings and queens and castles.

Two months into my royal romance, the Brit drove me to
my job at the Irish-American newspaper across from the Empire
State Building, and on our way, at a stoplight, an old woman
wearing a Glad Bag approached the jeep and asked the Brit for
money. Instead of ignoring her or saying "Sorry, not today," the
Brit jerked his car up and back and told her to fuck off.

Although he was sweet to me and bought as many gin
and tonics as I could swig down at the tiny bar we frequented,
Downtown Beirut, I started to lose interest in the Brit. The only
thing that really excited him was his catalogue of circular saws
and electric sanders, unlike Joseph, who raged about the CIA's
involvement in Central America and spit at stretch limousines.

While cleaning his marijuana pipe, I told Joseph I was getting
bored with the Brit; but I didn't tell him about Margaret, blonde-
haired, blue-eyed, Irish-Catholic Margaret, who I'd been flirting

with at work, where we'd cut out shamrocks and leprechauns and place them atop Irish pub ads, where together we'd roll our eyes when Pete, who always reeked of bourbon, commented on how nice our asses looked. I wasn't sure it was flirting, but I liked the tension, the way she rested her hand on my shoulder, the way she made me nervous, in a good way. She told me I was her role model, her hero, for having two cute boyfriends, for traveling alone in Europe, for inspiring her to plan her own European adventure.

A week later, Margaret and I drank White Russians and danced to Aretha Franklin's "Who's Zoomin' Who?" in my apartment and right before the song ended, she fell on top of me and we kissed and held each other and she asked if I had ever done this before.

Margaret and I spent the entire next day holding hands and kissing, right up until the sun went down, when I walked her to the subway and hugged her goodbye. Then I met the Brit, who escorted me to an East Village art opening, where artsy people in black outfits stood outside and drank champagne while Dominican and Puerto Rican kids rode their banana-seat bicycles in circles and screamed for their *abuelas*.

Saturday, I met my ex-roommate Amy for iced cappuccino and miniature canolis at Veniero's, where we talked about men, where I told her about the Brit and even though she never met him, she was happy for me, as she wasn't too fond of Joseph, especially after Joseph had punched a hole in her bedroom door when I beat him at a game of chess. Amy lived with her clean-cut boyfriend who we called "Pointy" because of his pointy features, a midwestern boy who worked at a fruit stand and snorted heroin.

When I saw Margaret next, at work, she told the office about the amazing date she had gone on the night before, a date with a law student, Brad, who she had so much in common with that it was "uncanny," a word she kept repeating over and over, uncanny this and uncanny that, and all the while I stared into the light box in front of me, slowly cutting out leprechauns and shamrocks and harps with an X-Acto knife.

Finally Margaret flew to Amsterdam and left me with her clean-cut frat-boy buddies to hang out with, but I preferred to spend time with Joseph, who one night told me that Bill Kane overdosed on heroin. Bill, who I had a brief fling with the year before, a filmmaker guy I had gone to college with, a guy my age with a life ahead of him, dead and gone. Bill, who, I later learned, shot up all the time and could have killed me too.

Surrounded by Kenny Sharf and Keith Haring paintings, the Brit and I waited for watered-down free drinks in exchange for our VIP passes at the Palladium, where I ran into a friend from college, a painter named Albert, who had recently returned from Europe and bragged about the thousands of dollars he and his new boyfriend had spent in only two weeks. When I introduced him to the Brit, Albert looked him up and down and nodded in approval, and as soon as Albert found out that the Brit was a carpenter, he hired him to do carpentry work at the art gallery he managed. So the Brit and Albert became friendly, perhaps too friendly, and two weeks later, Albert told me the Brit got wasted and stayed over at his house. "And by the way," he said, "the Brit's got a huge dick."

Rita came to visit and spent most of her five days in New York ignoring me and hanging out with anarchist and communist contacts.

When I ran into the Brit at the Pyramid Club, he hugged me, bought me a drink, and introduced me to his new girlfriend, a petite, blonde-bobbed French girl who made hats. I introduced him to Amy, who had just moved into a one-room studio sublet on MacDougal Street because she had broken up with her junkie boyfriend, Pointy.

One night I cooked dinner for Amy and we walked along the Hudson River, strolled down Christopher Street in the West

Village, and together we found women's bars, where, as soon as I
walked in, I giggled and calmed my nerves by swigging one drink
after the next. We met two or three times a week and walked and
talked and swigged drinks, and one night at a women's bar on
Sheraton Square, when we watched women slow-dance, I asked
Amy if she saw any cute women, and in response Amy stared at
me and said, "Yeah . . . you."

We left the bar and walked towards her apartment, where we
jumped around to Billy Idol's "Dancing with Myself" and ended
up holding each other. Amy still flirted with men and I still slept
with Joseph, who had no idea about Amy, but Amy and I talked
every day and continued to spend nights together.

Six months later, Albert and his boyfriend hastily left on
a night flight to San Francisco. It turned out that they'd been
dealing cocaine and paid a thug to beat up a young mafioso who
owed them money. Now, the Mafia men wanted to kill with a
vengeance.

Margaret had come back from Europe and invited me to a
party where she introduced me to her new boyfriend, a painter
from Poland.

After Amy threatened to date an actor boy, I called it quits
with Joseph and made a go at monogamy, a go at a committed
relationship with Amy, now that I wasn't sure about variety being
the spice of life.

Amy and I laughed a lot, composed music, improvised come-
dic skits about real estate moguls buying up the East Village, and
homophobic Polish waitresses who said, "The gays are disgusting.
How could they do such a thing?" Amy encouraged me to pursue
my artistic endeavors and hooked me up with an all-girls band,
Rapunzel. But something didn't feel right, and all the while, I was
in the closet about our relationship. Amy didn't understand why I
was so secretive. I told her I wasn't ready; I didn't feel comfortable
with the whole lesbian thing, not yet anyway.

Three years into the relationship, I agreed to go to therapy with

Amy, but after two sessions, I sublet my apartment for a month and left for San Francisco, where Paula created sculptures from neon lights and Jesus heads and wasn't yet worried about dying.

Upon my return to New York, Amy broke up with me and started dating a magician, a man she met while bartending at The Village Idiot, the tiny bar that used to be Downtown Beirut. Because of the poor economy and exorbitant real estate costs, just about every gallery in the East Village had closed down. Albert died, not from a gunshot wound but from AIDS. And Paula called to tell me about Barry, who just tested positive for AIDS.

Two days later, she found out she was HIV negative. She remained friends with Barry and often brought him bee pollen and Spirulina, until ten years later when Barry was too sick to take care of himself, when he flew home to Indiana where his parents took care of him until he died in 2002, when his parents honored his request to be cremated but didn't know what to do with the ashes. They sent them to Paula and, to this day, Paula's not sure what to do with them. "They're in a box in my closet," she told me.

But now it's 1989 and Amy just broke up with me. She didn't want to be the only one working on the relationship, and when I left for San Francisco, she had had enough.

So I am grieving and I don't even know if I like boys or girls and I find myself in the Cubbyhole, a lesbian bar on Hudson Street, dancing to R.E.M.'s "It's the End of the World as We Know It" with Robert, a tall, handsome, heterosexual man who lives around the corner from me. We exchange numbers and he calls the next day to invite me over for a chicken dinner.

The chicken is tender but my feelings for Robert are not—not in a romantic sense—yet we become buddies and he is more than willing to accompany me to lesbian bars.

One night Robert and I walk home from Cave Canem, a bar that was once a gay men's bathhouse but is now a trendy straight bar, except for Sundays when it's Girl's Night. And it's Sunday and

I'm tipsy and Robert and I walk along First Avenue with Kiki, a tiny Japanese woman who speaks little English. I feel hungry and want a burger, so we stroll into McDonald's and I get my burger and we sit down and I'm laughing with Robert and Kiki and then I start to choke and I can't breathe and I think, *Jesus Christ I'm going to die right here in McDonald's and would anyone believe I haven't stepped into a McDonald's in years*, and Robert asks if I'm okay and I shake my head from side to side and time stands still and Robert moves over and prepares to do the Heimlich maneuver.

But I cough up salty onions and live. And I leave McDonald's and walk out into the brisk autumn night and pass an old black man tap-dancing to "Tea for Two." I take a deep breath, then hug Robert and Kiki and walk towards my apartment. I don't know it at the time, but I'm happy to be single, happy to be healthy, happy to watch leaves chase each other in circles until they pause, until the wind shifts, until the leaves disband and scatter in all directions.

13

Women of Pompeii

Besides a longing to see the ruins of Pompeii, I didn't have any plans, didn't buy any guidebooks. I just wanted to get away. From New York. From not knowing what the hell I was doing with my life. From my relationship with Amy. I was terrified to commit to such a scary thing—being with another woman.

In front of the Kiev Restaurant, Amy and I hugged. "I'll write to you as soon as I get to Europe," I said.

My parents had no clue about my relationship with Amy. Once I invited her to my parents' house for a Passover seder. Towards the end of the evening, the phone rang and my mother called me into the kitchen. "Phone's for you," she said.

"Hi, my name is Bernie Cohen," a man's whiney ghost-voice said at the end of the line.

"I'm sorry," I said. "We're in the middle of a seder."

Like me, my mother loved to get lost in foreign cities, to walk through cobblestone alleyways, to discover exotic food in out-of-the-way restaurants.

On Mother's Day, a week before I boarded a flight to Frankfurt, my mother showed me pictures taken with her 110 Instamatic camera. Pictures from her recent trip to southern Portugal. We sat on the steps of my childhood home in Long Island, my mother narrating the blurry photos, one by one. "That's the little hotel we stayed at," she said, pointing to a slanted white building with a bright red door, a similar hue to her henna-dyed hair. I imagined her walking out the door, full of anticipation, ready to find a tiny café with a blaring television where she'd eat fried sardines and sip red wine.

Two days before I left for Italy, I phoned my mother. "I'll be back in a couple months," I said.

She let out an enthusiastic sigh, tinged with envy. In the background, my father yelled, "Why can't she get a regular job and stop running away?" He took the phone from my mother and said, "Why don't you open up a Carvel? Or better yet, become a speech pathologist."

When I arrived in Frankfurt, I bought a schnitzel and landed myself a seat on a night train to Milan. Four hours later, a blond guy hauling an oversized orange backpack in one hand and a guitar in the other pointed to the two seats facing me, jolting my body out of a deep sleep. "Speak English? Are these taken?"

I wiped my eyes. "I don't think so," I said.

After stowing his backpack away, he set his guitar upon his knee and plucked a few notes. "I'm Randy. From San Diego, California."

I sat up straight, introduced myself. "I'm from New York City." Outside the window, the clock at the Stuttgart train platform read 12:32.

"Never been to New York City," he said, then strummed a major chord. "Seems like a wild, wild city."

"Yeah," I said, slumping over and shutting my eyes.

But Randy wanted to talk. And strum. "Where you headin'?"

"Milan. And you?" An American flag was sewn onto Randy's orange backpack.

He played the first few bars of "Stairway to Heaven." "Not sure. I was thinkin' Zurich, but Milan sounds good too." He leaned his guitar against the wall, unfolded his map.

Randy plucked at his guitar all night and followed me to Milan.

Once there, I found a cheap hotel and went out for pizza with Randy. He talked excessively about his hernia operation. Everyone in the restaurant glared at us and shook their heads. After eating his last bit of pizza, he said, "It's gettin' kinda hot in here. Wanna go to the American Express office?"

Three years earlier, on the London-Manchester Express, I had met Francesca, a woman from Milan. She was envious of me because I lived in New York. Why do people have this romantic idea of New York? It's just a bunch of buildings and taxicabs. Her big brown eyes lit up. "Tell me," she said. "Have you seen William Hurt on the streets? I want to marry him." She seemed pleasant enough and gave me her phone number. Sometimes I think people give out their phone numbers as a souvenir of their conversation but don't really expect you to call. Like when you meet someone at a party and immediately connect, better than sex, and you get this idea that you'll surely become best friends but really, you know you'll never see them again. Perhaps in a dream. And maybe after a few months you see them walking with a friend and ignore each other, and pretend you never shared those intense moments in the kitchen by the pot of cold vegetarian chili. You pass by and want to hug each other but stare blankly ahead because things are too damn complicated. Just look in your address book. There's bound to be a few strangers lingering. Perhaps a few dead people that you don't want to scratch out, because then they'll really be dead.

I had one too many strangers in my address book, so I called Francesca. She said she remembered me. "What are you doing tonight?" she asked. "Do you want to come for dinner?"

When she opened the door, she stared, hard and curious. She had no idea who I was. I wanted to run. I swore to myself I'd never do this again. But what about that phone call? "You do look familiar," she said. "How do I know you?"

"I met you on a train. In England. I'm from New York."

Her face scrunched up. She didn't have a clue.

"We talked about William Hurt—"

"Now I remember!"

She smiled, hugged me, invited me in. She expected a different Lori. A woman from Switzerland. She thought it was odd that the person she expected had spoken English on the phone, when in fact the Swiss Lori was fluent in Italian. Isn't that like looking in a mirror and expecting to see your face but all you see is a tree, because in reality you weren't looking in a mirror, only a window?

The hors d'oeuvres that weren't meant for me were getting cold.

Francesca handed me a cheese cutter and kiwi custard tart. I couldn't gobble the food fast enough. Pepperoni, pate, broiled eel, vintage wine. We should all knock on strange doors every once in a while. Despite the fact that I wasn't who I was supposed to be, my host reassured me that she did remember me: "You are Jewish, right?"

Another bottle of wine uncorked, another kiwi tart. Instead of living in a roach-infested tenement flat like I did, Francesca's place was quite the *I Dream of Jeannie* paradise—red velvet sofas, plush Arabian carpets, clean white walls. And when I tilted my head up, I could imagine the curvaceous opening of a bottle leading to a cloudless blue sky. She told me about her job as an apprentice for a famous fashion designer; I told her about my job at the Irish newspaper.

She brought out a photo album of her travels. Pages of monuments and pigeons. There was even a blurry photo of me, red-eye glare and all, eating a Kit Kat on the train.

How many snapshots have sucked us in, made us into distinct background people? I've seen more than a few smiling men in my photo horizons. Some pose with a fist below their chin, others pretend to nonchalantly walk by, like an extra in an airplane movie. They want me to remember them. What they don't think about is that I have the power to decapitate them. Sometimes I do.

The doorbell rang. Francesca ran to her door. "*Ciao! Buona Sera!*"

A pudgy, bald-headed man in a three-piece suit stepped into her apartment. Francesca introduced me to her smiley-faced friend who squeezed my hand for a moment too long. He apologized for his poor English, gobbled a wheel of cheese, and soon drove off in his tiny sports car. It all made sense. She was his mistress.

The next day, I met Francesca's friends. I didn't know what it was, but they immediately embraced me. Did they want to practice their English? I was invited to vacation in remote country homes off the Mediterranean and feast on gourmet dinners in the mountains. One friend told me about her parents' farmhouse in Sicily, how we could ride around on their Vespa scooters. I anticipated tranquil evenings by the sea, drinking wine, watching fishermen hook worms to fishing lines.

I told my new friends I would call them after traveling on my own. I traversed Venetian canals, ate chocolate in Perugia, saw Michelangelo's *David* sculpture in Florence, talked to toothless old women in Cortona and made my way to Rome, where old men slowed their cars and waggled their tongues at me. After two weeks of traveling I had had enough of ogling Italian men. I wanted to speak in my native language, to speak to a friend, so I purchased a plane ticket to London to see my friend Marjorie.

Before leaving Italy, on a dusty June day, I made my way from Rome to Naples to Pompeii. Ever since my parents had shown me images of their trip to this preserved city fifteen years earlier, I'd been haunted by the toga-draped population in their last moments of life. I tried to imagine the terror, the panic before Mount Vesuvius erupted and mummified the city in a matter of seconds. With my Super 8 movie camera, I filmed petrified canines in corners, women praying with their arms outstretched, a shoemaker hammering a sole. I filmed the pastel-colored mosaics and panned to a cemented couple whose legs were still stretched with panic. I didn't connect the fleeting nature of my own life with that toga-draped population embalmed in plaster white.

Back at my Rome hotel, I had a vivid dream: a mob of Middle Eastern boys stood around a car and chanted. Flames shot up and eventually burned the car to nothing but ashes. I woke up in a panic, wiped the sweat off my forehead and pushed my thumping heart back in place.

From that day onward, official men in uniform were trying to track me down. Really. I cashed enough traveler's checks, so they couldn't track me down that way. Besides sending Amy a postcard about my trip to London, I hadn't written to anyone; I was too busy watching the stars quiver. You couldn't do that in New York. What a great feeling to have been anonymous among a foreign language, fog, and an open window. No strings, no commitments.

Two days later, Marjorie met me at London's Victoria Station. She hugged me, asked if I was hungry. I was starving. While making our way out of the station, Marjorie frowned, then sighed. "Your brother called last night. He found out from Amy that you were coming to see me. It's your mother."

A car crash—quick and painless.

In my head, foreign radio static blared a Japanese baseball game, a German call-in show, the Israeli national anthem, a Bulgarian chant. A cat-gut violin bow ripped down my spine. I could hardly stand. The same Middle Eastern boys from my dream chanted. Flames swirled and leapt and shot up around me. Smoke clouded the sidewalk. The daylight sky turned dark and ashy. I envisioned the women of Pompeii posed in toga-draped huddled embraces, forever mummified, another woman hunched over, holding onto her child for dear life. And I coughed, wiped the volcanic ash from my eyes, blew the blackness from my nose.

14

The Weight of Stuff

I sat on a cardboard box in my childhood home, one in a circle of many cardboard boxes. Amy, my girlfriend, sat to my left. Joseph and the Brit, two ex-boyfriends, sat across from me. On my right was Aunt Helen, an Auschwitz survivor. We were sitting *shivah*, a seven-day grieving ritual, for my mother.

Aunt Helen lived "underground" during the war, and throughout my childhood, I assumed she lived in a coffin-like contraption. I didn't know that "underground" was a term for "in hiding." Now the only person underground was my mother. She had been buried the day before. When I had learned of her death, big black cars were rolling out of a New Jersey cemetery.

Gladys Shapiro, the first person to greet me when I had entered the house, used to drive me to Hebrew school. She once shut the door of her Buick Electra 225 on my finger. I hadn't seen her in years. Tears flowed down her wrinkled face. She hugged me, said, "Such a loss. What a tragedy."

Following Gladys, my father threw his arms around my shoulders, the first and only meaningful hug he'd ever given me. "It's all my fault," he said, shaking his head. Before I had left for Italy, my father bought my mother a used Nissan Sentra. Once and for all, at fifty-seven years old, she was going to get her license. But before she had the chance to take the road test, they were on their way to a wedding when another car crashed into the passenger side of the Nissan and killed her.

My father had chauffeured my mother to meetings, work, shopping malls. He waited for hours in mall parking lots, sitting in the driver's seat, reading the newspaper. Although he complained, "The woman is wild! She buys clothes one day and returns them the next!" he didn't seem to mind his role.

At sixteen I got my learner's permit. While teaching me to drive, my father often screamed, "Brake! Brake! What the hell are you doing? Trying to kill us?" At this point, both my brothers had their licenses. My father bought them a beat-up yellow '72 Impala to share. As one brother drove on the highway, the other sat in the back and dropped lit firecrackers through the hole of the rusted-out car floor.

When I passed the road test at seventeen, I began to chauffeur my mother to shopping malls, the only place where we bonded—sort of—over the half-price clothing tables at Alexander's, amid the sales racks at J. C. Penney. She never asked about my personal life, not since junior high when she badgered me about why I didn't have any friends.

A year after I graduated from college, while shopping in Filene's Basement, I told my mother I was moving to Minnesota with Joseph. "We're leaving in two days," I said.

My mother, who didn't appear surprised, angry, or *that* concerned, said, "I'd like him better if he were Jewish." She continued to flip through the rack of pastel-colored sundresses.

"He could pass for Jewish, couldn't he?" I said, flipping through the rack too, trying to keep the momentum of distraction going. "His friend who lives in Minneapolis is paying for the truck. We're taking some of his furniture."

Always one for finding good deals, my mother examined a price tag, lifted the dress from the rack, and said, "Will his friend reimburse you for gas?"

"Absolutely," I said, eyeing the dress my mother held.

She hummed the theme from *MASH*.

While sitting *shivah*, we're supposed to disregard our own vanity, our own mortal bodies, and honor the life and spirit of the deceased. Mirrors are covered. Now, as I mourned the loss of my mother, I felt like I had the same expression as Aunt Anna who suffered from Alzheimer's disease, staring blankly ahead. I was too numb to cry. But I found a hand mirror in the bathroom drawer and examined the mole on my left cheek, now a raised bump. When stressed, the mole felt bigger, tougher. I hated my mole. I wanted to get it removed. In photos of myself, I saw the mole as the focal point. My friends told me I shouldn't worry about the mole, that it gave me personality. My mother had the same mole in the same place. She didn't mind hers.

No one knew Amy was my girlfriend, and I didn't correct friends and family when they referred to Joseph as my boyfriend. Grateful for Joseph and the Brit, they had made the trip out to Long Island to show their sympathy, to share in my grief. And it didn't hurt to have living, breathing proof of my heterosexuality.

Like Aunt Helen had been, I felt like I was underground, "in hiding." Although there were no Nazis ready to pounce on me if I was found out, in my mind, my situation felt just as dire. The thought of settling into a "deviant" life, a life without a husband and children, frightened me.

A week before I left for Europe, Amy and I argued outside the Cubbyhole, a women's bar in the West Village. "You're just embarrassed of me," she said, her arms swinging wildly around her Betty Boopish face. "That's why you won't come out."

I looked down at my new Doc Martens. "It's not that," I said.

"Then what is it?" she screamed. She flung her leftover Chinese container to the ground. A glob of lo mein splattered atop my right shoe.

With my shoulders raised, I stood silent, stone-faced, and started to cry.

Amy picked up the half-full container and threw it in the garbage. She sighed. "I'm sorry," she said, folding her arm into mine.

In my childhood bedroom, still covered in fluorescent orange and hot pink wallpaper with hippies flashing the peace sign, Grandma Becky sat on the bed, head in her hands. "Florence, my only child . . . gone," she said in her thick Yiddish accent, a language my mother knew as well.

I wrapped my arm around her shoulder. "I'm here for you," I said.

With her shaky fingers, she caressed her wedding band, twisted it clockwise, then counterclockwise.

My grandmother once told me she had never loved my grandfather. When she was sixteen, she met Grandpa Harry, both of them fresh off the boat from Russia, trying to make a new life in Montreal. Soon after their brief love affair, his family moved to Brooklyn, and two years later, when her family settled in Brooklyn, they reunited. But my grandmother didn't feel any passion when they met again. "I felt pressure to marry him," she said. "Because of this, I never was happy." A year after my mother was born, during the height of the Depression, my grandmother had an abortion. "We couldn't afford to have another child just then," she told me. But the abortion left her sterile. And while my grandfather pieced fur coats together in the garment district, rumor had it that my grandmother carried on an affair with his best friend. During the last years of her life, my grandmother's humped back would grow bigger, heavier, until her legs finally gave out.

My mother refused to part with anything. She held onto newspapers, broken bicycles, travel brochures, expired coupons, old clothes, baby shoes. Leftover birthday cakes from years past crammed the freezer shelves. Our two-car garage was piled to the ceiling with her possessions, including items she solicited as head of the rummage sale committee for two Jewish women's organizations.

My mother suffered from chronic asthma, a condition she developed after bearing her third child. Every so often when her lungs tightened, she'd gasp and hold her chest. When I was eight, she had a bad case of pneumonia and spent two weeks in the hospital. I prayed every day that she wouldn't die, that she'd come home soon. Once she was back on her feet, she roamed through dusty antique stores, buying up old medicine bottles, washboards, cake molds. And she continued to add to the mounds of old clothes and broken toys in the garage.

Perhaps my mother, the only child of immigrant parents, felt lost, in isolation, out of control, caught between different languages and cultures. I suspect that she found power in objects, that they made her feel grounded in time and place and, like a life raft, kept her afloat. Clutter is tangible, always there in times of suffering. It's weighty and takes up space, providing, perhaps, a false sense of security. After all, who would have taken pleasure in a broken Chatty Cathy doll? In a musty, moth-ridden pink dress made for a three-year-old? Feng shui experts believe that every object gives off energy, has its own history. Maybe that's why clutter piled high makes me nervous and antique shops frighten me. The collective force of all the objects is like listening to hundreds of staticky radio stations all at once.

When she married, my mother gave up her art. One of her framed blue and green abstract paintings hung in our living room, a testament to her younger years, before babies and a garage full of possessions. Perhaps to fill her creative void, she retreated into clutter, television, antiques, and shopping. When I showed her experimental photomontages I had made in college, she asked, "Whatever happened to those nice sunsets you used to take pictures of?" When I spoke about the possibility of going to graduate school for art, she raged at me, "You don't go to graduate school for art! You go for medicine or law!"

After I drove Joseph and the Brit back to the train station, Amy
spent the night in Long Island. We slept on the ground floor of
my house, in my mother's "Oriental" room. Japanese lanterns,
ivory figurines, and jade sculptures lined the redwood cabinets.
Upon the golden oval of carpet, Amy and I wrapped our arms
around each other and I got lost in her smells and curves, and I
clutched her as if I was in the middle of a violent sea and I had no
choice but to hold on.

The next morning, while Amy showered, my father sat in the
kitchen, nibbling on a bagel. He said, over and over, "Your friend
is cute. Maybe I should date her."

My sister, who didn't yet know about my relationship with
Amy, chimed in, "Imagine, Amy could be your stepmother."

I fake smiled and held tighter to my secret, repositioning
the burden—my imaginary refrigerator—so it didn't slide off my
back. I popped up from the turquoise kitchen chair and opened
our real refrigerator, hiding my welled-up eyes behind the door,
staring at the racks full of tiny red milk cartons, leftover milk
parcels from her class. One Halloween, when my brothers were in
high school, my mother suggested that instead of throwing eggs,
they could throw the containers of rotted milk.

After I dropped Amy off at the train station, I opened the creaky
but operable door of the wrecked Nissan Sentra, still in our
driveway. I sat in the passenger seat. A remnant of my mother's sequined dress, a pearl-lined purse, and matching silver
shoes lay idle on the floor of the mangled vehicle. I rummaged
through her purse and found a cracked mirror; in it, I saw my
broken reflection.

Following the seven days of *shivah*, I went through boxes of
coupons, maps, newspapers, put them in huge Glad Bags and
threw them to the curb.

I visited my mother's gravesite and added rocks to the top
of her tombstone. One rabbi explained that the material of the

stones is imperishable, as are our souls. Another Jewish scholar said that this is a symbolic act indicating that members of a family or friends have not forgotten the deceased. I found a small orange stone and placed it in the middle of the other stones. I thought of my mother's red hair; random strands clung to her purple wool coat, still hanging in my closet.

In her final years, my mother collected a menagerie of tiny crystal animals displayed in a glass case—among them a horse, a rabbit, a duck. I snatched up the duck and the octagonal mirror it rested on. Now they sit on my kitchen windowsill, along with other miniature animals I'd collected, some made of stone, others made of wood. When the sun shines on the duck, tiny colorful fragments of light sparkle on white walls, reminding me of a photograph I have of my mother at fourteen, her face freckled, her hair in braids. In it, she's holding onto a pole, smiling at her mother, my grandmother smiling back.

Nine years after my mother's death, a plastic surgeon removed my mole for a five-dollar co-pay. But two years after the surgery, a shadow of the mole resurfaced. Little hairs began to sprout from it. I'm comforted to know my mother won't leave me.

I am different from my mother. I never gave up my art. Five years after my mother's death, I enrolled in a creative writing graduate program.

I am different from my mother. She never got her license and ultimately died in the passenger seat.

Perhaps I'm more like my Aunt Irene, Grandma Becky's little sister. My aunt worked full-time at Macy's, traveled the world every chance she could, and never married. Out of all the relatives, Aunt Irene was the most vivacious, always smiling, singing along to her favorite song, "Those were the Days." But Aunt Irene died of a terrible autoimmune disease when I was eight.

In my last year of high school, I sifted through her slides: Aunt Irene in front of the Kremlin, on a Havana beach, pointing to the leaning Tower of Pisa. In one photograph, dated 1959, she's arm in arm with a Rita Hayworth look-alike in front of a '57 Chevy on Daytona Beach.

Six months before she died, Aunt Irene clapped to the scratchy *Fiddler on the Roof* soundtrack blaring from my grandparents' hi-fi console. "Dance, Lori, dance!" she said, a huge grin on her face. In a Brighton Beach high-rise overlooking the Coney Island skyline, I jumped around, leapt in the air, and performed unrehearsed pirouettes for a bevy of relatives. They clapped and cheered, and not quite sure what to do with the attention, I hid behind my mother and cried.

After Aunt Irene died at the age of fifty-seven, relatives *tsked* in her apartment that overlooked the Brooklyn-Queens Expressway. While scavenging through her possessions, her brother, Uncle George, said, "Such a beautiful woman. What a pity she never married."

"Plenty of men proposed, but no one was good enough," Aunt Anna said.

"And look what happened," my father said.

I am different from my mother. Antiques and clutter make me nervous. When I'm surrounded by clutter my chest tightens, my back hunches, I can't breathe. I'm allergic to dust, like my mother. But she still spent time in dusty antique shops and rummaged through junk in our mildew-filled garage. Every so often she had an asthma attack, some worse than others. During one attack, the day after my ninth birthday, she sat in our kitchen and held her chest and neck. Her face turned red. She eked in a breath and mouthed the words, "Find my inhaler. I can't breathe." No one else was home. I ran into her bedroom, searched through her pocketbooks and pulled out lipstick-smeared tissues, loose change, supermarket coupons. But no inhaler. Her gasps got louder, deeper. With my own chest tightened, I searched her purses again, thinking to myself *Please God, don't let her die, don't let her die.* Finally I found her

inhaler and ran back to the kitchen and handed it to her, and after three long sprays to her lungs, she took a deep breath.
And so did I.

15

A Certain Shade of Blue

My eighth-grade English teacher, Mr. Flannery, told our class, "By the time you're twenty-five, someone close to you will die. Someone you'd least expect." And then he told us about love, how he met his wife: "I blame it on fate. I had to meet her. It was part of the big plan." In class, we analyzed lyrics to pop songs and during our analysis of Joni Mitchell's "Chelsea Morning," Mr. Flannery closed his eyes and took a deep breath. "And the butterscotch stuck to all my senses. What an amazing metaphor!" I knew then the world was full of plans. Love and death and beautiful metaphors awaited me.

That year, I set up a darkroom and spent hours under amber safelight glow watching images of my poodles and nature and my naked sister come to life. On occasion, I overexposed the negatives and when I dunked the photo paper in the developer tray, the impression would pop up straight away and turn black within seconds. Just like that, light could turn to darkness.

I fixated on the idea of holding onto an instant, on manipulating moments by burning and dodging and altering light and temperature and time, on shooting images dead in their tracks. Arresting a moment, seizing it, containing it within an 8" by 10" border.

After printing a photo of my white pocket poodle wearing a light blue jacket, I made another discovery—a certain shade of blue, called non-repro blue in the graphic-arts world, disappears when translated into black and white. Thus, in the photo, my dog's jacket ceased to exist.

After my mother died, I wanted to understand death. To smell it. Taste it. Touch it. Through the Gay Men's Health Crisis, I volunteered to be a "buddy"—to help out and befriend a person living with AIDS. And so I met Nestor, an illegal immigrant from Ecuador, an Indian man-boy who could have passed for fifteen, but in fact, was two months older than me. We walked around the streets of New York City and I talked in broken Spanish and he complimented me on my accent and corrected my mispronunciations. One day, by the Hudson Street Piers, we sat and watched the water sway and listened to the seagulls squawk and stared across the river at the "Good to the Last Drop" Maxwell House sign in New Jersey. "Four years ago, I came to New York," Nestor said. "My dream. I found a job as a busboy in Greenwich Village. Then I met Ryan, a waiter. He's the only man I slept with, ever. I'm bisexual."

"So you've had girlfriends?"

"I slept with a prostitute in Quito." Through his black Chinese slipper-shoes, Nestor wiggled his toes. He moved his legs up to his chest and wrapped his arms around his knees.

I told Nestor about Amy, my girlfriend of three years. How I also considered myself bisexual. "I suppose if I weren't with Amy, I might be with a man."

"It's better that way," Nestor said. "More choice, no?"

A devout Catholic stricken by guilt, Nestor accepted his fate. Until his diagnosis, he had lived with his aunt in Queens, but her husband didn't want anyone with AIDS near his family. And when Nestor's immune system failed and he had to check into the hospital for a week, his uncle wouldn't let him return. Because he had nowhere to go, his home was now St. Vincent's Hospital. Finally, a Catholic Charities boardinghouse located by the Hudson River in the heart of the West Village offered him a bed.

At the time, the romance between Amy and me had already faded. Death kept us together. My mother's death. We held on to those last vestiges of a faded image, an image that could only be seen if you held it up to light at just the right angle.

In my sixth-floor tenement apartment, I showed Nestor photos of Amy. Amy and me dressed in babushkas, pretending to be Russian peasants. Amy and me dressed in black, pretending to be snooty gallery owners. Amy and me dressed in rags, pretending to be street people having a fight—she trying to steal a bagel from my hand, threatening me with a hammer.

During this time, the late eighties, ACT UP boys and (some) girls in knee-length dungarees and white T-shirts and Doc Martens boots and backward baseball caps held protests and kiss-ins and blocked streets, demanding that drug companies and government agencies focus more on helping people with AIDS, on finding a cure, on fighting homophobia, on rebelling against death and invisibility. They organized a protest against the Sharon Stone movie *Basic Instinct*, claiming that the film propagated homophobia. Every Monday at the Gem Spa newsstand on St. Mark's Place and Second Avenue, I bought a copy of the weekly magazine *Outweek*, a publication that reported the latest news in the gay community and outed gay celebrities and politicians. At night, activists posted lists of suspected gay people on telephone poles. I played lead guitar in an all-girl rock band, Rapunzel, led by Diane, president of the local Dykes on Bikes chapter. This was a time of rebellion and love and death in the age of AIDS. On a daily basis, I perused the *New York Times* obituary section. Along with the old, distinguished CEO men, I found write-ups about young men—artists and actors and choreographers, dead before their time. Although closeted to many, including myself at times, I attended ACT UP meetings at Cooper Union. Impressed and ignited by the rage, passion, pride, and creativity of its members, their kiss-ins, protests, and other actions (including one activist who disrupted Walter Cronkite's evening news and yelled on camera, "Fight AIDS, not Arabs!") sped up the government's testing and approval of safer and more effective drugs for people living with HIV and AIDS.

I showed Nestor a picture of my mother during her first year of college, her freckles and red hair shimmering in the sun, posing on the Coney Island boardwalk with her friend Shirley Goldfarb.

"You have the same face as your mother," he said. "Are you close to her?"

"She died earlier this year," I said. "In a car crash."

"I'm sorry," Nestor said, placing his hand on his forehead.

I never knew my mother. And then she was dead.

After a moment of silence, Nestor spoke about his mother, how he hadn't been back to Ecuador since he came to the States, how he missed her, how he couldn't go back now because the doctors in his country didn't have the knowledge and technology to manage AIDS patients. "But I wish I could see her," he said. "I love my mother."

I stopped myself from tearing up. "Do you have any brothers or sisters?" I asked.

"My sister Mari Paz, she maybe will come to visit me."

Two months later, when his sister did visit, Nestor showed her the track marks on his arm. "I've been using heroin. I got addicted," he said, when in fact the track marks came as a result of constant intravenous needles jabbed into his arm. But for Nestor, it was easier to come out as a junkie than a queer.

Nestor excused himself to use the toilet. When he needed to go, he always asked, not to be polite, but because he knew myths about catching AIDS from toilets still ran rampant. He followed up, "Are you sure it's okay?"

That day in my living room, I set up a tripod and camera and Nestor waited until I pressed the camera's self-timer and I ran into the photo and together we smiled and giggled and waited for the flash to go off. I took a bunch of photos, of us, of him alone, his striking Aztec face, his tender smirk, ready to take on the world, if only his immune system weren't a land mine ready to detonate.

Following a day of running from floor to floor at the department of immigration on Nestor's behalf—in order for him to continue receiving health care he had to obtain citizenship—I knocked on the door to the Catholic Charities home so I could return Nestor's passport.

A nun unlocked the huge wooden door and looked me up and down. "Yes?" she said.

"I'm a volunteer from Gay Men's Health Crisis. I've got Nestor's passport."

The nun's expression turned sour. She grabbed the passport and just about slammed that giant door in my face.

The next day, when I told Nestor about the interaction, he said, "They don't like the gays. On Pride Day, they took us to a park in Upstate. But when we arrived back, I got up on the roof of the building. And I watched the fireworks."

From the sidelines on Fifth Avenue and Tenth Street, Amy and I had watched the parade, starting out with the Dykes on Bikes and all the rainbow flags, and continuing with the sober queers, and gay and lesbian cops and firefighters, and the parents and friends of gays, and baton-twirling drag queens. People cheered and clapped and at one point towards the end of the long stream of marchers, Amy said, "Let's join in!" and she ran into the fray. Still contending with my own low-level rage against myself, I remained on the sidelines. A bulky deadweight in my heart.

Two weeks later, Nestor called from St. Vincent's. "I'm in the psychiatric ward with the crazy people," he said. "I don't know why."

I visited Nestor. A huge black man unlocked a steel door, a tiny steel-meshed window in the middle. On the other side, I stepped into hell. Blaring TV. Cigarette smoke. Patients walking circles mumbling and groaning to themselves. I asked to see Nestor. A nurse led me to his room.

"Lori," he said, getting up out of bed, leaving the copy of *People* he'd been reading on his pillow. "Why do they put me here?" Appearing levelheaded and out of place, he led me into the loony bin lounge.

A stringy-haired woman blew smoke rings towards the television, laughing to herself. "Why *are* you here?" I asked.

"I told my uncle I saw Mother Fatima on the subway. It was an advertisement. He told my social worker I was hallucinating."

I saw those ads too. A subway billboard. "Be Kind to Your Mother," the ad read. "That's why they put you here?"

Nestor shook his head, shuffled his slippers. "I'm not hallucinating!"

I called his social worker and explained the situation. Five days later, he returned to the Catholic Charities house. I later learned that sometimes doctors put people in the psych ward when no free beds are available in other wards.

After the loony bin lockup, Nestor's health deteriorated. Diagnosed with Kaposi's sarcoma, his disease began to make its external debut—his body became a canvas of discolored patches.

On a crisp, spring day in April, I met him by the Washington Square Park arch. He handed me a container of fresh blueberries. "There was a man selling them on the street. Very cheap. They look so good. You know, they don't have these in my country."

Although blueberries were my least favorite fruit, I thanked him, grateful for the sentiment. "How about I take you for an iced cappuccino?"

And with my blueberries in hand, we walked towards Café Orlin. I had planned on taking pictures of Nestor, but considering his condition, I kept my camera out of sight.

In her final years, I didn't take a lot of pictures of my mother. I didn't visit home often, even though it was an easy forty-minute train ride away from Manhattan. Going home reminded me of her detached presence. And my dead poodles—the only family members I could hold and hug.

Two weeks after Nestor's body broke out in blotches, he called from the Catholic Charities home. Whispering into the receiver, he claimed the nuns tried to poison him. "They're putting drugs in my cereal. They make me sleepy and weak; they make me hallucinate. Get me out of here."

"You think they're really doing that?" I asked.

"Get me out of here! Please!"

Days later, Nestor checked into the hospital for the last time. Two nights before he died, he struggled to sit up. He apologized for the sullied bedpan at the foot of his bed. Hanging above the bedpan, a tiny television blared an episode of *Gilligan's Island*.

I sat down on the chair next to the bed. "How are you?" I said, not knowing how else to approach a dying man.

"Not so well. But how are you?" he eked out. "You're sad, aren't you? You tell me what's going on, okay?"

I told him about Amy. She had broken up with me. "She was my family," I said. I stopped myself from saying more. Why burden Nestor in his last moments of life?

"You'll be okay," Nestor said. "It's okay." He lifted his hand and gripped mine. "Thank you for your friendship."

Nestor's funeral took place in the Catholic church attached to the boardinghouse where he spent the last six months of his life. I wondered if he had thought about his impending funeral taking place just steps away from where he lay down each night. Among the people at the sparsely attended service, his mother and sister sat in the front row, holding each other and moaning.

During the memorial, held in both Spanish and English, I stared at the small casket on display. And I prayed for Nestor, who didn't help me understand death, but helped me understand dying with dignity. And I prayed for his mother, who had last seen her son four years prior, en route towards his American dream.

And I cried for my mother. And I cried for Amy.

On the steps of the church, after the service, I walked up to Nestor's mother and told her Nestor was a friend of mine. I handed her an envelope of photos taken of Nestor, a healthy-looking Nestor, smiling for the camera, despite the fact that he was dying in a land far from his home. His mother pulled out the pictures and held them close to her chest. She hugged me, thanked me again and again.

And I walked back to my apartment, alone. Just six tedious flights to climb and a futon to cry on.

I opened my fridge, searching for something to eat, only to realize I wasn't hungry. That's when I noticed the blueberries Nestor had given me. They remained in my refrigerator for at least a month after Nestor died. Like a memorial candle, the blueberries paid homage to him. Everyday I looked at them. Until they were completely dried up. Until they transformed into little stones.

Before tapping the refrigerator door shut, I thought about blue. How a certain shade of blue, when translated into black and white, disappears.

16

The Last Days of Disco Donut (1987–89)

At the Irish-American newspaper where I worked, I met a tough Puerto Rican typesetter, Diana. I called her Diana Pequeña because she was little; besides, there was another Diana in the office, and that Diana was always on the telephone so I called her Diana Teléfono. Diana Pequeña and I would often lunch together and joke about a lounge called Carmelita's, a second-floor establishment above Disco Donut on the corner of Fourteenth Street and Third Avenue. For some reason, I thought Carmelita's was a massage parlor that doubled as a house of prostitution. Only years later did I find out it was a legitimate bar that held parties for gay women.

Instead of calling me by my name, Diana referred to me as "Nigger." She said, "Yo Nigger, what are ya getting for lunch today?" And I answered, "Las partes de pollo de su madre"—my Spanish translation for "Yo momma's chicken parts." With that answer, she stopped her typing and wailed with laughter. I know now that many social critics would consider Diana's use of the N-word downright wrong, but I looked at it as a compliment, a term of endearment—that's how she referred to her Puerto Rican buddies. So I thought, why shouldn't I, a white Jewish girl, be flattered by the title?

In addition to the Irish newspaper, Diana worked another typesetting job on weekends and was in the Army Reserves. Most of her earnings went into the hands of Pamela, her big black girlfriend whom she lived with in a crime-ridden section of the Bronx. On payday, Pamela would come up to the office to collect

Diana's cash, and as soon as she left, Diana would complain about Pamela's expensive taste in clothing, jewelry, and perfume.

But boy could Pamela cook. Once they invited me for a dinner party, and Pamela prepared fried chicken and biscuits and sweet potatoes and chitlins. Also at the dinner party was Pete, another typesetter from the office. He was a forty-something alcoholic ex-Beat with rotting teeth who often made crude comments about women's body parts. Because he knew how to combine just the right amount of wit, adulation, and charm with his sleaze (he recited Blake and wrote poetry), we all tolerated him. "You've got a great ass," he said to me, "but you've got to keep your back pockets empty." To make extra money, Pete let himself into the office late at night and used the equipment to set type for pornographic magazines. He made sure to retrieve his work before anyone found it, but on occasion he forgot. One morning, I found type about jisms and knockers and whips and orgies and knew it had nothing to do with the luck of the Irish.

"Hey Pete," I said, holding up the galleys. "You forgot something."

A minute later, our boss, who had a wooden leg, hobbled into the production room, lost his balance, and fell down. We all ran towards our soft-spoken, white-haired boss and hoisted him up.

When the boss hobbled away, I said to Pete, "So what do I get for saving your ass?"

"Holy bejesus!" he said, laughing. "How about a night in the sack?"

Pete's charisma and confidence helped him win over the heart of the newspaper's Ivy League–educated editorial assistant, Lynn. Although neither one acknowledged their relationship, it was an open secret in the office. Things appeared to be on the upswing for Pete—he stopped drinking, moved into a nice apartment, and had his own newspaper column. But while Lynn was vacationing in Florida, he phoned me on a Saturday night and begged me to meet him. "I've got a bagful of cocaine.

I don't know what to do with it!" he said. "I'm in your neighborhood, and I'm high as a kite!"

"I'm sleeping," I said. "Do you know what time it is?"

"But I've got a ton of coke! What should I do with it?"

I suggested he bring the bag to work with him on Monday.

Despite Diana's involvement with Pamela, Pete often burst
into homophobic tirades, especially when a gay Irish group
demanded to march in the St. Patrick's Day Parade: "What right
do they have to want to march in *my* parade? They have their
own fucking parade!" He concluded his rant with the obligatory
question: "What do those perverts do in bed anyway?" Eventually
he calmed down and tried to make amends by telling Diana how
great her ads were looking, or mentioning to no one in particular
how brilliant Oscar Wilde was.

The boss never caught wind of Pete's nighttime typesetting activities or his occasional sleepovers in back of the Xerox
machine (too drunk to go home), but his luck could only hold
out for so long. A couple years after I left the paper, he left five
frantic messages on my phone machine; he'd just been tested
positive for the HIV virus. Because I volunteered as a buddy for
people with AIDS, he thought I could help. "I'd been shooting
heroin three times a week for the last twenty years," he told me.
"I knew exactly when I caught the virus the second I slipped the
needle in my vein."

For a while, Pete went to an HIV-positive support group
"made up of 90 percent fags" and he ate well—brown rice,
steamed vegetables, bee pollen, and seaweed shakes. But despair
got to him; he resumed drinking mass quantities of Guinness and
tequila. Too ashamed to present his shriveling body, he left his
apartment only to go to the hospital.

The night before he died, Diana and I tried to visit him
in an overcrowded city hospital, but the receptionist said no
visitors—he was in the intensive care unit. We decided to take
a chance and walk past the guards like we knew what we were

doing and we kept walking and found Pete, his cobalt blue eyes staring a hole in the hospital ceiling, his respirator chest rising and falling. "I'm gonna miss you," I said, not sure if he heard me.

Four days later, Diana and I walked into an Irish funeral home in the Bronx. "Nigger, this is fucked up," she mumbled. Someone handed us a poem Pete wrote ten years prior, about death, transcending life. We looked at him lying in the coffin, finally at peace, but all I could see was Pete, lighting up another cigarette by the photostat machine, checking out my ass, telling me how I'm gonna be a knockout by time I'm thirty-two.

17

Mongrels of Salamanca

From my very first day in Salamanca, where I took a month-long Spanish course, I noticed Anna, her strong swimmer's body, her long blonde hair flowing from shoulder to shoulder when she spiked a volleyball across the net. We sat with each other in the cafeteria and instead of eating the food, we shaped it into characters and color-coordinated it and made up surreal stories about the potatoes and chocolate pudding and beef stew. Eventually we started tossing food at each other from across the table. Anna, from Frankfurt, spoke fluent English (along with seven other languages) and asked me about New York and talked about Tolstoy and Thomas Mann and Nabokov and Italian operas, and this alone made my heart quiver.

One day in my dorm room, I turned on my tape recorder and asked Anna what she thought about Hitler.

"I don't know what to make of him," she said, clutching a Shakespeare sonnet collection (German on one side, English on the other). "My grandfather tells me Hitler was a good man. He saved the economy. He built the Autobahn. But my teachers say he was a bad man." Anna folded her arms, sighed. "To tell the truth, I'm sick to death of talking about it." She shook her head from side to side, placed her forehead in her hand as if just learning about the death of a loved one. "I don't want to speak anymore about this subject."

I turned my tape recorder off.

Two weeks before meeting Anna, I had visited Auschwitz, the darkened barracks, the final set of train tracks where thousands stepped from crammed freight cars. I viewed the torture chambers, the piles of glasses and shoes, the tracks leading to the

Birkenau crematoriums just up the road. I walked in silence. The birds were singing. The grass was green.

I hadn't planned on visiting Auschwitz, but while backpacking through Poland, I learned it was an easy day trip from Krakow. Although I learned about the Holocaust in Hebrew school, the cold reality of it didn't hit me until that day. Afterwards, I couldn't stop thinking about the ovens, the photos of naked women on their way to the showers.

Before making my way to Salamanca, I stopped in London and bought a pile of books about the Holocaust including one about how the American government let Nazi scientists into our country, scientists who might help us outsmart the Russians. Another about imprisoned gay men who had to wear pink triangles and how the ones who made it out alive had Nazi lovers who snuck them extra food.

Even while studying past and future conjugations for my Spanish class, I couldn't stop thinking about Third Reich atrocities. So I interviewed German students. I held up my tiny Walkman microphone and asked them questions: What did you learn in school about the Holocaust? What do you think about it? Do you think something like this could happen again? Most agreed it was a black period of German history, that Hitler offered the Germans a way out of a sinking economy, and that German citizens had no idea what was happening.

After I put my tape recorder away, Anna said, "I love Woody Allen. I've seen his last film, dubbed in German." And then she asked about my New York apartment. "Does it have those fire escapes on the outside of the building?"

I told her about the East Village—the area where I lived, my sixth-floor walk-up tenement flat. How during the quiet of the day, the sun streamed in and lit up my mint apartment walls, and a mild scent of curry and cardamom and jasmine surged in from the row of Indian restaurants one block south. Besides the Indian restaurants, an amazing array of cheap eateries lay just outside my door: Polish, Japanese, Korean, Middle Eastern, Italian. And right around the corner was a Jewish bakery, Moishe's, where I bought apricot hamentashen—triangular shortbread cookies— from a tiny white-haired woman who had a Yiddish accent and a tattooed number on her arm.

But I didn't mention the tattoo to Anna. Or how I imagined what that woman's life had been like as a young Jewess, lining up for roll call at Auschwitz or Dachau, how she feared for her life, how she watched her friends and family vanish, how she found the strength to survive the camps.

The old woman would count my change slowly, say, "Thank you, *Dahling*," just like my grandmother. My grand-mother who, at the age of fourteen, boarded a ship from the Ukraine to Montreal, not knowing a word of English, only Russian and Yiddish.

I didn't tell Anna how at eight years of age, when I'd learned about the Holocaust, I ran up to my Aunt Helen, an Auschwitz survivor, and asked to see her numbers. My aunt looked down, giggled, and ignored my request.

But I did show Anna a few poems I'd written, one about black-and-white poodles strolling across magenta carpet in my childhood home, one about choking on a hamburger and almost dying in McDonald's. It had been a year since I'd taken my first poetry workshop. Before then, I scribbled down thoughts, kept a journal, wrote bad poetry but never considered myself a writer.

Anna stared at the words in my journal. "Do you know these are very good?"

I asked if she wanted to go to the town square after dinner.

She handed my poems back. "Only if you promise to show me more of your writing."

When I heard Anna's knock, I was reading about Dr. Mengele, the Nazi doctor whose experiments included brutal surgeries and various amputations of limbs. I threw the book

underneath my pillow and opened the door. For a moment, my
eyes locked with Anna's and a tingly sensation pulsed through my
body. She touched my shoulder, asked what I was doing.

"Studying gerunds," I said, "and the past perfect."

On our way to Salamanca's town square, I stopped to throw
leftover cafeteria grub to emaciated gypsy dogs, dazed and hungry bow-spined mongrels. All over town, one could find these
dogs resting underneath cars or hobbling along in packs, mere
carcasses in motion. At first the dogs backed away, suspicious of
charity, as if the food were the usual stones.

"Why are you feeding the dogs?" Anna asked.

"They're hungry," I said. Images of starved Jews staggering
through the Warsaw Ghetto rifled across my mind.

Anna put her hair up into a bun. She looked like a Clinique
model. "Could you imagine all the ticks and fleas on them?"

I threw another piece of food and a lone mutt crept toward it,
smelled it, gobbled it, provoking the others to hobble for a piece
of momentary salvation.

At the café, Anna and I talked about our respective profes-
sions. Ever since she was nine, she prepared herself for a career in
law. She looked forward to the day when she could have her own
firm. "So you don't have a job when you return to New York?" she
asked, perplexed.

I worked as a part-time and freelance design and layout artist, which, while it paid a decent wage, left me unfulfilled, empty.
Whenever I saved up enough money, I traveled. It was cheaper
to sublet my apartment and travel in Europe than to stay in New
York City. And on the road, I could avoid thinking about a career,
a subject that kept me tossing and turning and reaching for my
dead grandmother's bottle of Xanax at night.

Even though I didn't have a permanent job, I did have a
motley group of friends, many of whom I met the year before at
the Cubbyhole. That's where I met Robert. I enjoyed flaunting
the possibility of a union with him but couldn't figure out why

the reality of it turned my stomach. My straight, single friends envied my situation. One said, "If you don't want him, put him back on the market." Another said, "He's the last car on the heterosexual train."

Now, in Salamana's town square, Anna talked about the importance of a career. "You have to find stability," she said.

I imagined her in a starched Nazi uniform, her arm raised, saluting Hitler. I told her about my plans to travel around Spain for ten days after the Spanish course ended, how I looked forward to visiting Toledo, location of El Transito Synagogue, a former temple that had thrived five centuries ago, before the Spanish Inquisition.

"My parents have a Jewish friend in Paris," she said. "I stay with them when I visit." She looked at me and tapped by arm. "You know, one week after leaving Salamanca, I will intern at a law office. In Madrid." In a soft, sultry voice, she said, "So I could see you again before you leave."

Embarrassed about my craving to kiss Anna, I looked away. A filthy-faced gypsy child poured sugar from a packet into his mouth. Nothing about Anna's appearance made me think she was interested in dating women, but she exuded a take-charge energy—the way she walked into a room with poise and confidence, the way she questioned things. Her blonde hair, perfect skin, blue eyes, and fit body made her the perfect Aryan role model; no doubt, Hitler would have been proud. Besides that, she looked like the *shiksa* in my living room, the woman in the Lucite frame atop the never-tuned grand piano. Maybe I didn't want to be like the *shiksa*; maybe I wanted to be *with* her.

Anna and I never discussed two subjects: our romantic lives or the Holocaust. After talking about poetry, families, our travels, I went back to my room and read about the Nazis. One night I learned about the teenage girls who were promised an early release from the concentration camps if they volunteered to be whores in the camp brothel. Three months later, when they were all used up, they were led to a Zyklon B shower.

Each day Anna asked to see more writing. When I had no more to show her, she insisted I write more. With an audience of one, I forced out a poem a day. Two weeks later, she touched my shoulder and said, "You're getting better."

My heart palpitated. My arm hair sprung up. At the same time, I thought about those teenage girls in the brothel. A wave of nausea swept over me.

Towards the end of the Spanish course, when I could barely look in Anna's direction, she asked if I wanted to take a trip with her to Portugal.

"What are you going to do there?" I replied nonchalantly.

"Drink wine on the beach," she said, "and watch the sun go down."

Three days later, we zipped down country roads in her little blue Fiat and headed towards the Atlantic, where she stripped off her clothes and ran into the water. I looked away. We set up our sleeping bags, drank wine, and watched the sun go down. After she slipped into her sleeping bag, she thanked me for accompanying her.

"Thanks for asking," I said. With the full moon blaring, and my insane desire to kiss her, I didn't get any sleep.

In the morning, she awoke, looked at me and said, "I had these weird dreams. What do you call them, wet dreams?"

"You mean sex dreams?" I said, embarrassed that maybe she picked up on my thoughts.

We ate breakfast and drove on, watching old women in black walking alongside mules. Anna played a tape, Lisa Stansfield's "This Is the Right Time," and told me how the song reminded her of a crazy girl she met in a lesbian bar.

My ears pricked up. "What about this woman?"

"She was following me around all night. Finally I told her I wasn't interested."

The tension in her tiny car thickened.

Anna asked if I wanted to stop and tour a cathedral. "It's supposed to be very beautiful inside."

And so we walked through the incense-laden structure and she pointed out the Virgin Mary and Joseph and Jesus and all the lambs too. And I listened to every word intently, my eyes fixed on Anna's lips.

We bought wine and cheese and bread and had a picnic in an out-of-the-way cornfield. Then we set up our sleeping bags and tried to nap. We each had a book to read but after a minute I moved closer to her. And she to me. I dropped my book. And so did she. We leaned into each other. And kissed. And held each other. In a Portuguese cornfield. And I caressed the muscles in her arms, her neck, and she gripped my shoulders, ran her hands through my hair and maybe ten minutes later, she whispered, "There's a man walking in our direction." *Might the man be a police officer? Will we get caught and get sent away?* Anna suggested we ignore him. So I tried to stay calm and he ignored us and we continued to kiss and when we took a break, she said, "I didn't think you were a lesbian."

I lifted my head up. "I am now!"

During the next week, I traveled with Anna and we ate elaborate meals and slept on beaches and held hands. One night, in a cheap hotel in Lisbon, she read Shakespeare sonnets to me in German.

I asked if her friends and family knew she was a lesbian.

"They don't need to know," she said. "My mother asked me once and I denied it." She rolled her sleeve up and stared off in the distance.

Before leaving me at the Madrid airport, we kissed in a bathroom stall and cried. Her tears tasted like mine. Anna plucked a hair from my head and put it in her wallet. And there I was, falling in love with a woman who encouraged me to write more poetry and apply to graduate school. And she talked about wine and art and literature with great ease but refused to talk about the Holocaust and wasn't sure if Adolph Hitler was such a bad man.

For the next year, Anna and I continued our romance from across the Atlantic. We spoke by phone, wrote love letters, and when we had time off, visited each other. During that year, I read every book I could find on the Holocaust. One night I read a book by a Jewish Hungarian doctor—Dr. Mengele's assistant—whose job was to perform autopsies on gas victims. The Hungarian doctor spoke about a fifteen-year-old girl who survived the gassing and was led to him afterwards, wrapped in a blanket, shaking, scared, and confused. The doctor gave her a bowl of soup, tried to talk to her, wanted to save her. But after three days, the girl was led back to the chambers. "She'd talk," said Dr. Mengele. "She knows too much." I put the book down. I wondered what Anna would say to this girl if she had worked with Dr. Mengele.

I gave up on trying to make sense of the Holocaust.

Anna visited New York during Gay Pride Week. I mentioned a movie I wanted to see *Europa Europa*, a film based on the true story of a Jewish teen who joined the Hitler Youth in order to save his life.

She shook her head from side to side. "I refuse to see another film about the Holocaust!"

A car alarm wailed through the window. Perhaps her grandparents overlooked the smell of burning flesh in favor of a freshly paved highway, but I had my own blind spots to contend with.

That night, Anna tried to kiss me. I turned away.

The next morning, on our way to the Gay Pride Day Parade, Anna broke up with me. "I don't have time," she said, "to wait for you to be successful with your career."

I nodded and said nothing. Two balding men in leather and chains strolled by.

On the sidelines of Fifth Avenue, the two of us, in silence, watched marchers wave and cheer. Among the marchers: Radical fairies and gay college students and dykes on bikes and gay Christians and the original Stonewall activists and a contingent of Columbians pushing a huge coffee cup on wheels. At noon, everything got quiet. A moment of silence to remember the dead. Victims of AIDS. Afterward, foghorns went off. ACT UP activists raised their fists and placards in the air. "Fight AIDS! Act up!" they yelled. On their placards was the slogan "Silence = Death." A large pink triangle hovered above the words, the same triangle gay male prisoners wore as identifying badges in Nazi concentration camps.

Anna stood silent, her arms tightly folded. The stream of activists continued to chant. One marcher handed out pink triangle stickers. Anna folded hers and put it in her pocket. I took the backing off of mine and pressed it down on my shirt, just above my heart.

18
Feminist Christmas Tree Farm

On my thirtieth birthday, a week into my residency at a feminist Christmas tree farm, I asked Amelia and Jane, two other residents, if they wanted to split a dose of magic mushrooms a friend had given me. I'd done this sort of thing a handful of times; not for years, but it was my birthday and it was autumn in upstate New York and I was with two new friends. We mixed the stinky-foot-smelling dried flakes with strawberry yogurt and then walked outside, taking in the leaves trembling crimson on aspen trees. I held out my arms and said, "Look at the sun! Look at the trees, they're saying hello!" Amelia laughed, asked if I was for real. We walked to the pond, located next to the resident quarters and I slithered my body onto a chaise lounge and watched Sue, a poet who had a fondness for fixing Snapper mowers, slink out of the pond. She then placed each leg through an underwear hole as if she rehearsed it a thousand times before for my silent camera. I laughed tears like I never saw anything funnier.

The owner of the farm, a well-known feminist who bought the land with money made from her best-selling book of feminist criticism, asked if we had seen the farm manager. I couldn't speak. Instead, I giggled. Jane stuttered something about seeing the manager in passing. The famous feminist walked away, shaking her head.

The sunny sky darkened. Amelia and Jane disappeared. Alone in a strange place, with strange women drifting in and out of sight, I walked to the back deck of the resident's house, high on mushrooms, and sat Indian style in the drizzle. And I cried huge tears, tears that wouldn't stop. For what seemed like hours, I mourned the loss of my mother, the mother I wish I had known.

The mother I remember was off in another world—watching television, out shopping, humming to herself. To make matters worse, when I finally heard the news, my mother had already been eulogized and buried somewhere in New Jersey. I wondered why she had once looked at a silkscreen print I made for her and said, "I would have liked gold hoop earrings instead." Why, when I was a child, she had shopped for carnival glass and trivets in antique stores for hours on end while I cried, pleading for us to get out of those dark, musty shops piled high with ornate armoires and ticking clocks and antiquated dresses worn by women long dead. Why she'd bring home leftover milk containers from her kindergarten class until our refrigerator and freezer were jammed with them and when I opened the freezer, the parcels fell at my feet like little land mines.

And now it was my thirtieth birthday, and I was alone, weeping, saying to myself, *I'm so fucked up. I need to go to therapy. My life is a mess and my mother's dead.* Why, now, had her presence loomed so large? I prayed my father wouldn't call to wish me a happy birthday, because then he'd say something about how there was still time to sign up for the postal clerk test, or that I should become a psychiatric nurse.

I had read three autobiographical books by the famous feminist and admired her gutsy, honest writing about bisexuality, art, and love. So when I learned about her farm, I applied for a residency. In exchange for working five hours a day—trimming trees and painting and mowing—residents received free room and board and time to work on their own creative projects. Before leaving for the farm, I sublet my New York apartment for six weeks and boarded a train en route to an idyllic wonderland full of smart women and sweet-smelling balsams, a place where Simone de Beauvior had visited before she died, a place where I could write poetry. Yet after working in the fields for five hours each day, I didn't have much energy to write. But I did learn about astrology from Amelia, a recent Harvard graduate. She made Japanese lanterns from thick paper, thin pieces of wood, and watercolors. At times Amelia made me nervous, in a good way. Maybe she liked me. Like that. I wasn't sure if I liked her back, like that, but I did like the attention.

One night I told her about my mother, so she deliberated upon my mother's astrological chart, calculating years and moons and suns and seventh houses. At last she jerked her head up and looked me in the eye. "It makes sense," she said. "She was meant to die when she did." She caressed small circles on my back. I didn't want her to stop.

On the first night of the residency, after a dinner of steak and potatoes and wine, I sat in on a conversation between Amelia and Jane, a striking Italian-Chinese Yale graduate who brought her husky named Sacco. "Where did you go to school?" Jane asked me.

I told them about the small state school I attended, located just north of Manhattan.

"Never heard of it," Amelia said.

They continued their conversation about Ivy League schools and social registers. About Ivy League friends they might have had in common. Never fully conscious of class difference before, I felt intrigued by these Ivy Leaguers, and at the same time, shunned for being a middle-class kid from Long Island whose parents weren't fancy lawyers and doctors, but schoolteachers who taught in Queens.

Two weeks into the farm experience, Amelia rode her Snapper mower up to mine. Over the rumbling engines, she screamed, "Do you have any water?"

I turned my Snapper off and handed her my bottle.

She swigged the water, looked at me, turned her Snapper off and handed the bottle back. "I have a crush on you," she said.

A gnat buzzed around my head. The idea of a relationship with Amelia terrified me. I said, "I like you too. But I think we need to keep this a friendship."

"Okay," Amelia said. She started up her Snapper. We both drove off into the midday fields to mow lush green pastures.

With short dark hair and perfect posture, Amelia had a presidential wife's aura like Jackie Kennedy, the type of girl every Ivy League mother would love her son to bring home for Thanksgiving. But she'd never had a girlfriend and I didn't want to be her experiment.

Back on the porch, still high on mushrooms, I wondered if my mother would approve of my relationships with women. She came of age in the fifties and in one photo during that era, she's with a gaggle of women friends in the college cafeteria, smiling a natural smile, a sketchpad and milk container on the table in front of her. In a later photo, she's sitting next to my father, our black poodle on her lap. Her smile is fake, strained.

My mother and I had one thing in common—our love of travel. But we traveled differently—I'd get a standby flight and roam foreign territories without a plan; she signed on for seven- or ten-day package deals. With great reluctance, my father accompanied her. And every time they returned, he said, "The woman is wild. Always running. Clomping like a horse."

Instead of pursuing the life of an artist and rebel like the famous feminist, my Brooklyn-born and bred mother got married, gave up her art, had four children and moved to the suburbs. She wasn't part of any consciousness-raising groups, but she was active with Hadassah and ORT, two Jewish women's organizations.

For a good portion of the time, the famous feminist tended to her dying mother, but the farm manager, Patty, a fiftyish heavy drinker and smoker who lamented over a biker chick who stole her heart ten years earlier, took over the helm. She lived in a trailer just left of the pond, and it was in this trailer where Jane, Amelia, Patty, and I watched the Anita Hill-Clarence Thomas trial. Jane, who had considered applying to law school, gave up-to-the-minute assessments. "I can't believe it's come down to pubic hairs on Coke cans!" she said. "Clarence Thomas is clearly guilty."

Patty nodded her head in agreement and broke open a new bottle of Smirnoff to mix with her tonic water.

When she did come back to the farm, the famous feminist brought with her a cloud of paranoia, fear, and guilt. At the dinner table, she often obsessed about money. One night, she ripped open the heating bill. "How could we have used this much gas in one month?" she asked. "Who's turning the heat up?" We all looked down. "I'm going to have to start charging for room and board."

We all knew part of the reason for the exorbitant bill. While the heat blasted, Jane left the front door open. Her dog liked it that way.

Later that night, the residents sat on Jane's bed in the chicken coop to discuss the famous feminist's treatment of us. "It's not like we're freeloaders," said Sheila, a woman who just finished her PhD in plant biology and on the first night accidentally wiped herself with poison ivy after peeing outside. "We all work hard. She's getting free labor!"

"It's like she's an intruder in our blissful world," said Amelia.

"And she makes us feel like we're the intruders!" Jane said.

"Maybe she's just stressed about her mother," I said.

"Maybe she's not taking her drugs," Sheila said.

"I'd rather be here than in Manhattan," I said. "It's beautiful."

During one meal, the famous feminist said, "I did my part in the feminist movement. Now it's your turn."

We lowered our heads, feeling ashamed that we hadn't started up any activist organizations.

I enjoyed the attention Amelia gave me; she critiqued my writing, cut my hair, asked me to teach her guitar chords. Together we sang the farm manager's favorite country song, "Come Next Monday." We danced around with power tools singing "I've Got the Power."

So the day Amelia rode up on her Snapper and said she had a crush on me, I wasn't surprised. But after I rejected her, she barely acknowledged me. When I spoke at the dinner table, she hummed and stared out the window. Like my mother.

I don't want to say I was trying to work out my mother issues with Amelia. I don't want to admit I fell into the push-pull trap, but once she pulled away I wanted her like never before. Like a drug. I gave in. We kissed.

Amelia and I took walks in the fields and watched deep crimson and yellow leaves flutter to the ground. She said, "You're my woman." I smiled, not sure what to make of the situation. After all, Amelia never had a girlfriend. She wanted a girlfriend and there I was. As long as I held my heart at bay, Amelia tugged at it, refusing to accept only part of it. "You need to let go and trust," she said.

I squeezed her hand. Afraid of exposing myself, of getting hurt, I couldn't let go. I looked up at the Douglas firs. "How long does it take for a Christmas tree to grow?"

When I returned to Manhattan, Amelia stayed with me in my small one-bedroom apartment, then found a four-month sublet on the Upper East Side. Through a friend, I found freelance work at a publishing company, designing and laying out textbooks. Despite the recession, perfect-postured Amelia had no problem finding high-paying computer work.

Amelia, who spent her childhood on a farm in Vermont, felt overwhelmed by the city's crowds, siren shrills, and desperate men in ragged coats begging for spare change. She cried for these men. She cried for the bearded homeless woman who wheeled around a huge canvas cart filled with old newspapers and ragged clothes, topped off by a live duck. And she cried for what she perceived as our relationship in a past life. "We were married," she said. "You were a man. We had a terrible argument and then you were killed in a car crash."

And she cried when we held each other, when she looked into my eyes and said, "You're holding back. You need to let go. You're not giving me your whole heart."

Two weeks before Christmas, as a favor to the famous feminist, Amelia and I returned to the farm to help sell Christmas trees. A constant stream of customers showed up with saws in tow, ready to cut down a tree of their choice. In the sub-freezing weather, we greeted families, offered them hot cider, pointed them to fields of full-grown Christmas trees to inspect. Despite my blue fingers and toes, I felt pleased to see the fruits of our labor pay off. At night, with other former residents and friends of the famous feminist, we ate a hearty meal of turkey and stuffing and sweet potatoes, celebrating a day of hard work and record tree sales. Just before we clanked our wineglasses together and toasted to the famous feminist, I wondered if my mother would have felt comfortable at the table.

When we had gotten together, Amelia came out to family and friends. With her prodding, I began to open my heart. I told her about my fears of abandonment, of living as a gay woman. Yet with each offering, Amelia backed away. That's how it worked. An exhausting game of push-pull. And then she told me of the demons that haunted her, how she wanted to go to India and pray at a monastery. While sitting on my futon, she broke down and wept. "I'm from another planet," she said. "From Uranus."

"Huh?"

"I need to talk to a psychic," she said.

I ran to Enchantments, a new age witch store down the block and found a newspaper with advertisements for psychics. Amelia spoke to one in Colorado who asked to speak with me. "Imagine a bridge made of diamonds," she said. "Connect it from your heart to Amelia's."

Even a bridge made of diamonds couldn't keep us together. As soon as I gave Amelia all of my heart, she became obsessed with k.d. lang and moved to San Francisco. Perhaps subconsciously I knew that the more I gave, the more she'd pull away. And if I gave all of my heart to her, she'd finally free us both.

I visited Amelia in San Francisco. On our last night, she broke up with me. She wanted to be on her own. She needed to work on father issues. She needed to work on past life regression. I held her and cried, just like I did a month into our relationship, when we had driven up to her grandmother's farm in Vermont. Once there, we walked in the woods and snapped photos of each other by Amelia's favorite willow tree. We looked at old family photos with her grandmother. That night, in a small farmhouse bedroom, we lay next to each other. Amelia turned the light off. Five minutes later she asked if I felt anything weird in the room. I knew that she meant ghost-weird. I clutched her body and started to shake.

"No," I said, an attempt at denying any weirdness in the room. "What do you mean?"

"Don't freak out," she said, "but your mother is trying to speak to you through me."

While I shook and gripped Amelia's body in that Vermont farmhouse, she told me my mother wanted me to know she was okay, that she loved me, that I'm going to be okay, that I shouldn't worry about her. Following a long pause, Amelia asked, "Do you want to say anything to your mother?"

"Tell her I love her."

"Anything else?"

I continued to tremble and cry.

A few moments later, Amelia sighed. "It's gone," she said. "The presence is gone." She turned the light on. "That was really weird."

I looked at her face, her dilating brown eyes, wanting so much for that encounter to have been real.

Now, while we held tight to each other in San Francisco, our last night together, I lifted my head from Amelia's shoulder, wiped my snotty nose and thanked Amelia for leading me to a world where the dead don't care who you love, a world where I could imagine my mother—the artist and traveler—at the table, celebrating another day of communal spirit and record sales at the feminist Christmas tree farm. We'd pour wine and hold up our glasses. My mother would clank her wineglass against mine. "*L'Chaim*," she'd say. "To Life."

19

The Girls of Usually

During my first semester of grad school, I met with Allen Ginsberg every Thursday night to discuss my poetry. One night I brought him a cryptic poem about my girlfriend, Maria.

"Is this about a man or a woman?" he asked, twirling a tuft of his gray beard.

"A woman," I said, almost ashamed.

"So you like girls? Or are you bisexual?"

I wasn't sure why I felt so uneasy discussing my personal life with a flaming fag. "I guess bisexual."

"When I was younger, I slept with a lot of women," he said. "That's the only way you find out who you really like to be with."

Perhaps I felt nervous because I was talking to an American icon, or because we were in a mint-green classroom, or because I felt ashamed I was with a woman, or because I wasn't sure why I was still with Maria. She and I had argued about her drinking, we argued about the half-truths she told me, we argued about her close friendship with a woman who bought her compact discs, household appliances, and often wined and dined her at fancy restaurants.

Maria, a native of Mexico City, had been awarded a year-long, postdoctoral fellowship to study the brain's elasticity and its relation to memory. In a windowless lab near Washington Square Park, she performed experiments and designed computer programs. While she studied graphs about short- and long-term memory retention and which hemisphere of the brain remembered what, I wrote poetry about my childhood and dead poodles and vague declarations about my ambivalent sexuality. One teacher said, "The unspoken, the white space between the lines, is

just as important, or more important, than the words themselves."
Sometimes I wanted to get lost in that white space.

Despite our proximity—Maria lived in the West Village and I
lived in the East Village—we sent each other two or three e-mails
a day. In one e-mail, she wrote of the frustrations and doubts she
had about her research project. In response I told her to think
positively, to recall the articles she had already published, and at
the end, I said, "Thanks for your love. I can't wait to hold you and
hug you and kiss you." I pressed Send. To my horror, the letter
was sent to my brother on the west coast. My brother who knew
nothing of my personal life.

I called Maria. "What should I do?" Sweat streamed from my
armpits.

"There's nothing you can do," Maria said. She suggested I
write him a follow-up e-mail. "Tell him he may receive a letter
that wasn't meant for him, but to disregard it."

My brother replied: "Guess the letter wasn't for me, but it was
pretty interesting." Despite the door that flew open because of
an unexpected gust of wind, the door that could have led to an
honest exchange, I didn't walk through. I didn't say, "Yup, I have a
girlfriend. She's a scientist, like you. Does it freak you out?"

Funny how, in retrospect, I felt more comfortable discussing
my personal life with Allen Ginsberg than with my own family,
even after a computer glitch did the initial job for me.

But Ginsberg had no secrets to hide, not from the world and
not from a frizzy-haired, reserved student who wrote cryptic
poems. One evening, just before he critiqued my poem, he picked
up an official faculty rulebook from his desk and opened to a
page about how faculty shall not, under any circumstance, engage
in sexual conduct with a student enrolled in his or her class.
Ginsberg tossed the booklet aside. "Sleeping with your students is
the best thing you could do for them," he said.

He was an irreverent icon who didn't give a damn about what

people thought. The poet who had written, "America when will we end the human war? / Go fuck yourself with your atom bomb. I don't feel good don't bother me." Another night he talked about his financial situation, how for the first time he could finally live off his poetry now that he got paid thousands of dollars for readings. "But what's the point?" he said. "I can't even get it up any more."

I first met Maria on a freezing winter night at the Cubbyhole. Wearing cuffed Wranglers and lace-up leather half-boots on her narrow feet, she looked like a short-haired version of Frida Kahlo, minus the mustache and unibrow. All night she drank rum and Cokes and rolled her own cigarettes. "The drinks keep me warm. I don't like the cold," she said. She took a long drag on her cigarette, tilted her head upwards and exhaled a skinny ray of smoke. "It don't get this freezing in Mexico, ever."

Just four months before, I had traveled to Mexico. "Compared to Mexico City," I said, "New York is on Valium."

Maria smiled wide, a beautifully sad smile.

I told Maria about the smashed-up car that I saw slip off the back of a tow truck. "The driver just left it there," I said. "Right smack in the middle of a Mexican highway."

"It's like that," she said. "It's crazy. People do whatever they want to. The police don't care. They get the bribes. They don't have the rules."

A week later, we shared a taxi to her friend's party in Brooklyn. I noticed her eyeing my hairy leg, just above my sock. "I need to shave my legs," I said.

With her index finger she stroked the hairs. "I like it that way."

Her lack of subtlety made me nervous.

At the party, I met a group of women she referred to as "the girls of usually"—a core group of friends she knew from Mexico, all working without green cards, all fearful of the dreaded Immigration Man who might one day deport them.

Later that week, Maria sidled up to me by the jukebox at
Crazy Nanny's, a women's bar. She asked me to recite a poem.
"I don't know any poems off the top of my head," I said.
"What's on the top of your head?" she asked.
"My hair."
She caressed a lock of my hair. "Beautiful hair." She tried to
kiss me.
I pulled away. "I want to get to know you," I said.
"What do you want to know?" she asked.
I felt like an actress in a poorly written B-movie.
A friend of Maria's, an obese woman with a clubfoot and
thick glasses, walked towards us, aided by a cane. Maria introduced us. Carla limply shook my hand, looked above my head,
and hobbled to the bar.
"She's in a bad mood," I said.
Maria shrugged her shoulders, rolled her eyes. "But I'm in a
good mood," she said, touching my arm, "because you are near
to me." I stepped away to study the jukebox selections. When I
turned around, Maria held out a drink for me. "You like the gin
and tonics, don't you?" After she made a toast to health, money,
and love, we clanked our glasses together. "May you have all
three," she said, pronouncing *tree* instead of *three*.
Maria gave me a tour of her lab, the computers, the complicated machinery. She attempted to explain her project about
the brain in more detail, but I got lost in technicalities. Yet I was
impressed with the passion she had for her research, and even
more impressed that she had just come from a yearlong research
project in Paris. Pretty inspiring for a woman from a third-world
country, a country where the poor live in refrigerator boxes on
the outskirts of town.
After the lab tour, Maria led me to her Bleecker Street apartment, around the corner from the lab, a studio apartment facing
the World Trade Center towers. In her white socks, she skated
across the shiny wooden floor, arms raised above her head. She

sang "Waters of March" in Portuguese and told me about how some New Yorkers treat her: "First they ask if I'm Brazilian, if I'm Italian," she said. "When they find out I'm Mexican, they no longer are interested. Here, they hate the Mexicans, not like in Paris."

But I didn't feel that way about Maria. To me, she was an exotic and mysterious mad scientist.

After we kissed, I asked, "So what's wrong with you? You seem perfect."

She smacked her lips. "You'll find out, *poco a poco*. It's better to find out little by little."

A month into the relationship, I noticed that Maria spent at least two evenings a week with Carla. Not once had I been invited along. When I asked why the three of us had never gone out together, her shoulders hunched up. "What's wrong with having my own friends?" she said, clearing an *American Heritage Dictionary* from her kitchen table.

"Why are you keeping us apart?"

"She doesn't like to see us together," Maria said, tossing the dictionary onto a pile of psychology textbooks. Two books fell on the floor. "It makes her uncomfortable."

I tried to pick up the books, but Maria got to them first. "So Carla's in love with you?" I said, our eyes meeting.

"It's not my fault. I can't do nothing about it." Maria placed the books into a neat pile. "I'm not going to leave you for her. Don't be worried." She sat on her bed and slapped the space next to her. "Come here *mi novia*."

I plopped down next to her and nuzzled my head on her shoulder.

"You don't be so jealous," she said, wrapping her arms around my body.

Maybe my jealousy was getting to me. But then again, wouldn't the situation be clearer if Carla were a guy? If I were a guy? If a guy bought presents and wined and dined my girlfriend, and didn't want to acknowledge our relationship, wouldn't that be a problem? Yet when women are the key players, a sense of lawlessness comes into play. The unspoken rules bend like light through a prism.

When I wasn't angry about her relationship with Carla, I focused on Maria's drinking. Once I said, "You stumble home all the time. Why do you drink so much?"

"I'm just having a good time," she said. "I like to loosen up. What's wrong with that?"

No matter how much she drank, she was in the lab the next day, a serious scientist and scholar. And she always phoned to say good morning, to see how I was doing, to tell me she missed me and how her heart ached to see me again.

But as sweet as she was, I often caught Maria in lies, half-truths. One night she told me she planned to work all night at the lab, but the next day, she slipped up and mentioned she had gone out drinking. I got riled up and focused again on Carla. "She's in love with you!" I said.

"It's not my fault," she said. And then she showed me an article she was working on and asked if I'd correct the grammar. I shifted gears and saw the mad scientist at work.

Since Allen Ginsberg and I both lived in the East Village, we shared a gypsy cab home from Brooklyn after our poetry tutorial. One night, an inexperienced driver picked us up. "How do we get to Manhattan?" he asked.

Ginsberg gave directions. "How long have you been driving a cab?"

"This is my third day," the driver said. "But I've never driven to Manhattan."

"Where are you from?" Ginsberg asked.

"I'm Bengali," he said, swerving from one lane to the next. Drivers honked at us. They gave us the finger.

Ginsberg asked the driver if he knew of a certain Bengali poet.

The driver looked at Ginsberg in his rearview mirror. "Of course I know him! I've read all of his books!"

Ginsberg said he'd been to Bangladesh and had read poetry with this Bengali poet.

"What is your name?" the driver asked.

"You probably never heard of me. Allen Ginsberg."

"Of course I know you! I can't believe this! Allen Ginsberg! You are famous!" Now the driver was looking at Ginsberg in the back seat; our car nearly sideswiped the car next to us. More drivers honked and gave us dirty looks. *This is it. I'm going to die with Allen Ginsberg. It'll be my claim to fame. When I looked to my right, a yellow cab driver waved his arms and mouthed profanities. I made deals with god: Let me live and I'll treat myself better. I'll write everyday. I won't play Maria's games anymore. I'll tell her I can't deal with her relationship with Carla.*

Ginsberg chanted a song in Bengali. The driver smiled and looked at the road in front of him every now and then. Ginsberg turned to me. "Do you think you could write a haiku about this?"

I fake laughed. *Dead. I'm going to die with Ginsberg. Maybe my name will make the front page of* The New York Times.

But we made it to the East Village. I walked home, my body sweating. I dialed Maria's number. Busy. Dialed again. Busy. For the next hour, I later found out, she chatted with Carla. When I finally got her on the line, I felt weak, furious. "I almost died," I told her. "In a cab with Allen Ginsberg."

"I'm sorry, baby," she said. "I'm glad you didn't die. That would be terrible."

"I need a drink," I said. "Could we meet for a drink?"

"Carla is on her way. She's taking me out to dinner."

I walked across town to the Christopher Street Piers and watched the water ripples swish up and back. I attempted to let my anger, my frustration about Maria's friendship with Carla go. After all, I was a poet. I was alive.

Besides "the girls of usually," Maria hated to mix friends; she feared people would talk about her. One night we played billiards with a group of her friends, and at the end of the evening, they invited us out to play the following week. Maria already had plans but I agreed to meet the women. Maria fumed. She rolled one cigarette after another.

"What's the big deal?" I said.

"Find your own friends," she said, licking a piece of rolling paper.

Another Mexican standoff. Why did I stay with this woman who continually evaded the truth? Perhaps it was the way she said, "You don't love me. Tell me the true." She never raised her voice. She was such a sweet liar.

One night, I participated in a poetry reading at a crowded downtown café. At the conclusion of the reading, Maria and her friends disappeared. Two hours later they showed up at my apartment. I felt enraged, abandoned. Maria threw out flimsy excuses: We couldn't find the car; we couldn't find a parking space; we couldn't find a bank machine.

The next day, I noticed filtered cigarette stubs in her ashtray, not the kind she smoked. Empty beer bottles lined her kitchen table. "Where did those come from?" I asked.

Maria emptied the ashtrays, wiped her table with a rag. "Before I went to the reading, I met Carla," she said.

"You told me Carla doesn't smoke."

She picked up the bottles off the table and washed them out. She half-smiled and looked away.

"Where did these cigarettes come from?" I said, pacing around her kitchen table.

"I can't tell you," she said. She sat down, wiped her forehead.

I sat down next to her and took her hand in mine. "Why can't you tell me? You need to tell me."

"Because I can't," she said. "You won't like it."

Finally she told me "the true." After the poetry reading, she invited friends to her apartment, where they drank and snorted lines of cocaine. For the past four months, Carla had been buying it for her. Twice a week, they snorted it, a gram a week.

"What a great friend she is!" I said, glad to have nailed Carla and Maria, as if I were a lawyer finally getting the accused killer to fess up. And with that guilty verdict, I came up with an ultimatum. "It's either me or cocaine." I was pretty sure I meant it.

"I can't stop now! I need to have a little," she said. "Just a little before I quit."

We negotiated for hours. I walked towards the door. "You can have Carla. You can have cocaine. But you can't have me!"

She threw her body in front of me, blocking my arm from opening the door. "Please don't go!" she said. "I need you. I'll stop. I won't do it no more. When Carla comes tomorrow, I'll tell her I can't do it."

And with this disclosure, we cried, clutched at each other. In the middle of the night, she grunted and kicked her legs. I asked her what was wrong.

"I dreamt that a shark was eating my legs," she said, "trying to swallow my whole body."

Now that I pulled Maria's body out from a shark's mouth, I was nothing less than a savior. Me and Jesus and Mother Teresa.

The next time Maria saw Carla, she told her I had found out, that she had to stop snorting cocaine. Carla decided to quit in solidarity.

Little by little, *poco a poco*, I learned about Maria's upbringing, how her father had lived a life of lies. Six months into our relationship, Maria told me she had visited her grandparents in Florida before coming to New York. The story went like this: Maria's mother worked as an *au pair* in Brooklyn one summer. On the Coney Island boardwalk, her father spotted her mother, a fetching eighteen-year-old Mexican. He spoke fluent

Spanish, told her he was also Mexican but had been living in New York. Soon after, they married. Within the year, Maria was born. Her father lived under a Mexican alias when all the while he was a New York Jew, a fact her mother didn't learn until after Maria was crawling on parquet floors. Until she was five, Maria grew up on the Upper West Side of New York. She spoke fluent English, but eventually her mother left her father and, taking Maria with her, moved back to Mexico. Maria lost her father. She lost her English. For many years, the conman traveled back and forth from New York to Mexico, trying to woo back her mother.

While we watched dogs frolicking in the Washington Square Park dog run, Maria said, "I'm half Jewish. Like Frida Kahlo. You know her father was a Polish Jew?"

I wanted to know more about Maria. "Why did your father have to live under an alias?"

Maria scratched her nose. "I don't know. Maybe he already was married." She looked down, clutched my hand with her free hand. "We don't talk about it." She hadn't seen her father in years. "I hate the man," she said. "Last time I talked to him, I had just started university. I told him I was studying science. He said, 'We don't need any more women scientists. We already have Madame Curie.'"

In a sloped-floor midtown tenement flat overlooking a floodlit gas station, we spent Christmas Eve with the "girls of usually." There, we ate spicy chicken molé, drank beer, exchanged gifts, and danced to Madonna's *Immaculate Collection*. On the subway back to Maria's place, our knees touched; we looked at each other and grinned.

But I hated Maria for going to a party at Carla's on Christmas Day, a party I wasn't invited to. I hated her for lying about not having the ability to control the heat in her apartment, the sweltering heat that dried me out. "I like to sweat," she said. Yet at winter's end, I discovered a camouflaged-into-the-wall control box where one could flick a tiny silver knob to cut the heat off.

"Did you know about this?" I asked.

She looked out the window. "Do you want to get whitefish salad on a bagel? I love whitefish salad."

I hated her for accepting presents from Carla. I hated myself for the lack of rules I endured in our relationship, just like in Mexico where, Maria told me, cops were paid to look the other way. Or paid to look the wrong way. That's why three of the "girls of usually" had fled Mexico to escape murder charges.

Five years earlier, Maria's best friend, Mona, had invited her for Easter Sunday. But Maria had other plans. On Mona's terrace, Mona and three friends drank margaritas. By the end of the day, Mona was dead. She had fallen off the terrace. Family and friends were devastated. Six months later, Mona's mother, not able to accept that her daughter was dead, accused the three women of murder. Because the mother was a rich doctor, the three women were guilty until proven innocent. The women went to jail. The trial went on for weeks. Lawyers and expert witnesses proved their innocence. But soon after, the mother demanded a retrial. Instead of going through the ordeal again, the women fled the country.

In the back of my mind, I knew that Maria would return to Mexico after her fellowship ended, that our relationship would naturally end after the year. But Maria applied and received another six-month fellowship. Six more months wouldn't be that long.

But six months could be a very long time. Especially after a friend told me she had seen Maria in a long, passionate embrace with another woman on the street. When I confronted Maria, she said, "I knew she'd say something." Following a crying match, Maria agreed never to see the woman again. We played cat and mouse—she came out of the hole to taunt me, and when I caught her, she convinced me to do no harm, to let her go back in the hole so we can start the game again.

So why did I stay? No one wanted to be alone during a cold, gray New York winter. Or maybe it was the way Maria smiled and sang Spanish children's songs while slicing papaya. Or maybe it was the sadness in her eyes when she mentioned a brother, a brother I hadn't heard about before.

"He disappeared," she said. When she was fifteen, Maria had plans to meet her brother at Mexico City's anthropology museum. But he never showed up. "My mother hired a detective but after a year, they couldn't find him. They gave up."

"What do you think happened?" I asked.

"A lot of teenage boys disappeared around that time." She rolled a cigarette and spoke of aliens and perverted men and sex rings.

Maybe I stayed with Maria because her brother was kidnapped, or her best friend fell off a balcony and died, or because her father was a conman who lived under an alias.

Or maybe I stayed because I told myself half-truths. I convinced myself that if I moved to Mexico with Maria, I could get a job teaching English, she'd cut her ties with Carla, and we'd live happily ever after.

In the meantime, I continued to lie about my relationship to friends and family. I brought Maria home to Long Island for Thanksgiving. This is my friend, the Mexican doctor.

I finished my master's degree and, without Maria knowing, started applying to doctoral programs. But I could only keep the secret for so long. When I told her about my intentions, Maria hung her head and said, "Why do you need a PhD in English?" And when I was accepted into a program, we both knew the jig was up.

Before Maria returned to Mexico, we cried in each other's arms, as if we were both losing a piece of ourselves. We agreed it was best to let each other go, that if we found someone else, it would be okay.

When she arrived back in Mexico, we continued to correspond two or three times a day. In her e-mails, she asked why love was so painful. She insisted that I tell her immediately if I met someone else, that she wouldn't make a big deal about it but she had the right to know.

Yet three weeks later, Maria let me know she had kissed a woman. The e-mails got shorter, less frequent. And then she told me that she had a new girlfriend, Blanca.

I'm glad for you, I wrote back. *But right now I need silence between us. I need time to adjust.*

And just like that, our relationship came to a halt.

We still correspond now and then, updating each other on our lives. Maria continues to perform research on the brain and its function to memory. She is still with the same girlfriend. Recently, in an e-mail, I asked if she could send a photo of her and Blanca. A week later, she sent an e-mail with five attached photos—photos of her Labrador retrievers.

I found it odd that she sent pictures of her dogs rather than her girlfriend, but I also felt sad, sad that Maria still leads an evasive life. But who am I to talk? Despite the many visits with my brother and his family in Seattle, we never discussed my personal life or the letter that I accidentally sent, not until fourteen years later, when he found a version of this story in an online magazine. And he wrote.

> Perhaps I could have been a bit more engaging in my response to that errantly routed e-mail you refer to in your story . . . by saying something that would push beyond a lighthearted response, and more deeply into your personal life. Perhaps that was indeed an opportunity to pursue more discussion. I'm guessing that I was trying to avoid being pushy as you had never brought anything up with me directly about your sexuality, given your comfort level with that— even if you had been clear in communicating in implicit ways—and my sense is that we both understood the implicit communication. I've always felt that you would figure out if and when you wanted to share more with me about things, that I shouldn't necessarily take the initiative on pushing on

that. Although that email was a while ago, my sense is that it
was likely the case that I didn't want to put you on the spot,
and so I closed with an attempt to say, perhaps in too coded a
way, "not to worry—it's okay."

In our e-mails, Maria and I have reminisced about the good
times we had in New York with "the girls of usually." Somehow
all the heartache, the alcohol and stumbling, and the threats
have washed away in our memory, leaving us feeling a fondness
towards each other. In one e-mail, I recalled a ride we took on
the Coney Island Cyclone, the speed whipping our bodies down
rickety tracks, me laughing hysterically while Maria yelled over
and over, "*Ay Dios Mio!*"

As with love, there's a certain lawlessness to memory. At
times it protects us. At times it controls us. At times it needs to be
given a slap on the behind for letting us get into stupid situations,
over and over again.

Funny how certain moments lodge in our minds—the
confused, teary-eyed expression on Maria's face at Kennedy
Airport when she turned back one last time to say goodbye; my harrowing gypsy cab ride with Allen Ginsberg, him
turning to me, asking if I could write a haiku. A week after the
cab ride, along with Ginsberg and other students, I read two
of my poems at a poetry reading in honor of Walt Whitman's
birthday. The next day, I told Ginsberg how much I liked the
new poem he had read. He looked at me askance. "You were
there?"

When I read my poems, he was busy doodling, in his own
world, as we all are, I suppose, thinking of one memory or
another, as if each memory were a film that you watch in a darkened theatre, over and over, until the film's emulsion is scratched

thin, until footage gets caught in the projector's sprockets and bubbles up and dissolves under a smoldering bulb, until it's spliced back together, retouched, recreated, until the original film is altered into a mere apparition.

20

The Lost Language of Lox

Dear Sherry:

We met in a fiction-writing workshop, both of us doctoral students at SUNY Albany. You wrote stories about drunken escapades: one that took place on a Pepto-Bismol–colored bus in Nantucket, another about a marine who lured the narrator into his pickup truck and tried to pull off her shirt, but she ran, leaving one of her sneakers in his possession. Soon I learned there was nothing fictional about your stories.

Once the class ended, we bumped into each other in the university parking lot. "Let's drink whiskey together," you said. "Sounds like fun," I said, thinking, *How sweet. A young, cute, all-American, blonde girl wants to be my friend.* Even though you were a devout Christian, you wore a Star of David around your neck. I asked you why, and you said you believed in the Jewish roots of Christianity. And you loved Jewish people.

We began to talk on a daily basis. You told me about your boyfriend of five years who studied marine biology in Indiana and wanted to marry you. You said, "Maybe I'm in love with him but I just don't know it. I rarely see him and only call him when I'm drunk."

I told you about my relationship with my last girlfriend, a Mexican scientist who studied in New York for two years before returning to Mexico. At last, I spoke openly about my sexuality instead of hiding it. In response, you said you'd never been with a woman but had crushes on women, and added, "Any woman who says she hasn't thought about it is a big fat liar. Oh my gosh! I'm not hitting on you."

I didn't think of you as girlfriend material. You had a boyfriend. And you liked to drink. A lot. Besides, you were a practicing Christian and I was a lapsed Jew.

When we met for Sunday brunch, we both ordered bagels and lox and spent the morning talking about the connections between lox and love. "It's pink and soft, like a heart," I said. "And they're almost spelled the same."

The next day, you e-mailed me:

> oh my goodness . . . another similarity between love and lox? If you write loxloxloxloxloxloxloxloxloxloxloxlox, it looks like x's and o's. I haven't figured out what the "l" would be all about, though. Oh . . . maybe it's like the number, 1, so it could mean "one hug kiss one hug kiss," and all the ones would add up to lots which are sometimes involved in love. I like that.
>
> lox
—Sherry

A week later we took a day trip to Williamstown, Massachusetts. I loved driving in the car with you, listening to the mixes you made for me, both of us singing at the top of our lungs to Joni Mitchell, Cat Stevens, the Indigo Girls. For a good part of our visit, because it was raining, we sat in a combination café and photo lab. "What a great idea," you said. "You can drink coffee while waiting for your pictures!" I loved your optimism, your enthusiasm about everything, even a simple café. At the time, I had no idea about your ongoing depression. In fact, your cheerful disguise was so effective that a depressed classmate pulled you aside one day and said, "You give me so much hope. You're the happiest person I've ever met."

Two months into our friendship, my feelings about you shifted. *Did I like you? Did you like me? What about your boyfriend?* We spent more and more time together—sober time—playing guitar and singing, sharing our writing.

Since I didn't own a television, you brought your TV to my apartment. We watched Barbara Walters interview Ellen DeGeneres, the week before Ellen came out on her own show. We slouched on my futon sofa, our legs stretched on a milk crate, both of us drinking water. "Water is so good!" you said. "What a great idea!"

After filling your water glass for a third time, I sat at least a foot away from you, making sure not to get too close. But when the show ended, you slumped your body towards mine. I moved away. You moved closer and this time I couldn't help but lean over and kiss you. For the next hour, without saying a word, we kissed and held each other. Before you left, I asked what was going on. With a nineteen-inch TV in your arms, you said, "Whatever it is, it feels good."

That night I had a dream about an orange stray cat. The tiny stray had a drippy, gray, almost glued-shut eye, but when I bent down to pet the cat, the cat's eye fell out and transformed into an iridescent sphere of bright reds and blues and yellows, like a beautiful glass marble. I wondered if the cat represented you. Was I taking in a stray?

Together we spent time reciting poetry and plays, talking about writing and feminist theory, playing Scrabble. You offered insightful feedback about my writing and asked to see everything I'd written. Sometimes we'd write together and read aloud what we'd written and, always, you inspired me.

Three weeks into our relationship, at a martini party, you stumbled from one person to the next, telling each person you loved them. After six months, I noticed a trend; at parties, you drank and drank and drank until you sat in a corner and cried. So when a group of friends planned a party at a century-old house in the country, a sleepover party, a place I'd never been, I was hesitant to go. But we went and you drank and drank and when you ran out of cigarettes, you insisted I drive you to get more. When I refused, you demanded my car keys. You cursed at me and ran out to the road. "If you're not going to take me to get cigarettes," you wailed, "I'm going to hitchhike."

I chased after you, but you got to the road first and stuck out your thumb, just in time for a white Mack truck to stop. The door

swung open. You lurched into the passenger seat, but before you
had the chance to close the door, I ran up to the rig and pleaded
with the driver not to take you. The engine vrooomed and idled,
and the mustached man in a green plaid flannel shirt eyed you,
then me. You attempted to pull the door shut, but the truck driver
leaned over and pushed it all the way open. "Go back to your
friend," he said. "I ain't taking you nowhere."

You ran out of the truck, back to the house. I thanked the
driver. He could have raped you, cut your body into a thousand
pieces, gagged and drowned you. But he let you go. He let you go
back to the old house where you sat in a corner and cried. When
I sat next to you, you laid your head in my lap. You wept, shook,
apologized. I stroked your hair, calmed your trembling body.

And I wondered why I stayed with you. Was it the language
we had developed together? Our playful conversations full of non
sequiturs, starting with, let's say, lox and lint, shoes and schnau-
zers, moving onto eggplant and Toyotas, and ending with dolphin
squeals in Brooklyn?

And after sleepless nights of obsessing about my dead mother
decomposing somewhere in New Jersey, you held me, told me
that everything was going to be okay. "Your mother is so proud of
you," you once said. And when you smiled, the right corner of your
mouth slid up towards your cheekbone and took up half your face.

According to your Evangelical Christian parents, you were in the
grips of Satan for loving another woman. How could this love
that brought you so much happiness be the same love that caused
you so much pain and guilt? Now you drank at least a six-pack
every night. When you were good and drunk, you called Take-
Out Taxi, a food delivery service, and binged on chicken wings
dipped in blue cheese, cheese fries, ice cream. Once a slender ath-
lete, a rower for your college crew team, now you were a round-
faced chubby girl. You hated yourself.

Your guilt reminded me of my own feelings of inadequacy,

of going to family events with cousins, their kids doing the hora, my ninety-seven-year-old grandmother asking if I'd met a special man, my father trying to set me up with a police sergeant. "He's Jewish," he said.

On the nights we didn't spend together, I wouldn't hear from you until two or three in the afternoon, when you woke up. Until you called, I worried you were covered by a morgue sheet. At your apartment, I couldn't ignore the dishes piled high in your sink, floating in vomit. I rinsed the dishes, swept the dust bunnies out of the corners of your room. As your alcohol dependency worsened, you rarely made it to your job on time, if at all. You couldn't stop bingeing on food. I did what I could: I offered to go to AA with you. During a therapy session, I pleaded with your therapist to do something. "If Sherry continues like this," I said, "she'll be dead within the year."

Two years into our relationship, I accepted a full-time professor job in North Carolina. I wasn't sure how you would fit into my new life. After all, you were still in school. You were still drinking. At this point, you couldn't go a day without alcohol. In fact, on some nights, you'd swig down a twelve-pack of Budweiser, no problem.

The night before I left for North Carolina, you drank six beers, one after the next. On your couch, you plopped yourself down, apologized, and passed out. I pulled your sneakers off, put a blanket over your body, a plastic bucket by your head. I sighed, glad to be leaving, to be starting a new life in a new city, a life of shiny wood floors and white walls and Southern drawls.

Yet I missed you. A week into my new life, you phoned me at work. "I don't know how I got home last night," you said. "I remember drinking lots of Long Island iced teas at a bar. I blacked out. I'm scared. What if I was raped or something?" This time when I suggested you go into rehab, you didn't balk. You packed your bags and checked in the next day. Finally I could

relax. I didn't have to worry about you having a head-on colli-
sion. And I began attending Al-Anon meetings. I learned about
detaching with love, about the need to take care of myself.

A month later, you left as a sober woman. I was proud of you.
You gathered the strength to tell your parents to back off about
your sexuality. And they backed off. But you still suffered from
guilt and depression. We spent hours on the phone talking about
your alcohol urges, your depressive thoughts. By the end of the
school year, I felt drained. Finally, I found the courage to end our
relationship. But I assured you that you could still call anytime,
that I was your family, and I'd always be there for you.

I flew back to Albany to help you celebrate your one-year AA
anniversary. Your friends and family attended. We all listened to
your story of overcoming alcohol. We rejoiced afterwards at your
parents' home. Although they never accepted our relationship,
they always treated me with respect and even gave me a Yankee
Candle for a house-warming present.

Three months later, the day after Christmas, I called and
called your apartment with no response. Finally at two in the
afternoon, when you could no longer ignore the ringing, you
picked up and mumbled that you hadn't slept for the past three
days. You told me you took fifty melatonin capsules the night
before; you didn't want to wake up. I imagined your body lying
flat, your delicate hair matted atop your head. "Even with the fifty
melatonin," you said, "I couldn't get a wink of sleep."

It turns out that two days before, at your family's home, your
favorite uncle handed you anti-gay pamphlets: *When Passions Are
Confused*; *Rebelling Against God*; *The Natural Course of Things*.
That night you opened a pamphlet, read a few lines, and cried
into a pillow. You decided your sins were too much to handle.

You decided to check into a psychiatric rehab. By the end of
your stay, you felt stronger. Within months, you lost all the weight
you had gained, got a full-time job working with mentally hand-
icapped adults, felt more in control of your life. You joined a sup-

port network of Christian lesbians and began to feel proud of who you were. You felt anger, and then compassion, towards the people who judged you. You finally found compassion for yourself.

Six months later, we attended the wedding of a mutual friend in Vermont. We drove up the New York State Thruway while singing Ani DiFranco songs and making up chants about your schnauzer, Sherlock. Although our romance was over, our friendship had deepened.

A year later, you met Dena, a Jewish architect. Four years later, I made a toast to you and Dena at your commitment ceremony. Even your parents wished you a happy life together.

Yes, you still have your moments of feeling like a sinner, but you tell me you're happy. And I'm happy for you. You've come a long way since we met. I remember one night, a year into our relationship, when big tears had rolled from your eyes. I pulled my car over to the side of the road and asked you what was wrong. "Life's too hard," you said. "What's the point if I'm in so much pain all the time?"

I held your shaky shoulders. "Imagine happiness," I said. "Imagine what it looks like, feels like."

"I can't imagine ever being happy," you said. "It's not part of my universe."

There are days when I have a hard time imagining my own happiness, days when I call you to seek out answers, when you listen, give nonjudgmental advice, pray for me when my vision is clouded by muffled shades of gray, grays similar to the eye of the orange cat I dreamt about just after we met; the sickly eye that transformed into a sparkling sphere of color, the eye that has reflected your wisdom, wisdom I hadn't noticed at first, wisdom that helped us unearth a lost language of lox, a language instinctual as salmon swimming upstream, fluid as blood pumping to the heart, and we all know you can't change the direction of blood.

With love and lox,
Lori

21
Death and Furniture

My heart fluttered when I heard Lita belt out Patsy Cline's "Crazy" during a crowded open mic night at a local pub. In response to the audience's enthusiastic applause, she smiled humbly, then sat at my table and asked where I was from.

"New York."

"The City?"

"New York, New York," I said, almost stuttering. "I moved here last year. For a job." I gulped down my beer.

Lita pulled her chair closer to mine, combed her hand through her long blonde hair. She told me she had grown up in Arkansas and now worked as a lawyer.

"I'm a doctor," I said, taking note of her big blue eyes, her milky-white complexion. "A professor."

"Are you now?" Lita said. She picked up her beer bottle and clinked it against mine. "It's nice to meet you, Professor."

I didn't need any tricks to get Lita's attention, only to cultivate my coyness. Relieved and liberated, just out of a relationship with Sherry, why was I so quick to flirt with a new woman? Why do politicians send out happy promo shots with their families? Is this a sign of stability and commitment? Hence, without a family one is a wild card, unstable, a freak?

On our first date, Lita treated me to drinks and a fancy dinner at the local country club. Over the course of the night, she drank two gin and tonics, a glass of wine, and a beer. I tried not to notice, but after Sherry, I was on alert. On our second date, I mentioned my observation. In lawyer defense mode, she tried to put my mind at ease: "Five drinks in five hours," she said, punctuated by a giggle. "That's one drink an hour. Along with dinner, that's nothing!"

I was skeptical but let it slide. Besides, she was beautiful, smart, and my friends convinced me to give her a chance. I loosened up. I had to trust, just like a magician's assistant needs to trust the magician once she lies down in the coffin on stage. She needs to trust he won't saw her in half.

I told Lita I wanted to buy furniture, real furniture, so on our third date, we paid a visit to Haverty's Fine Furniture. As soon as I entered the store, I realized why I hadn't purchased any substantial recliners, armoires, or end tables: furniture scares me. It didn't help that at every turn in the crammed showroom, over-eager salespeople handed out brochures featuring bulky dining room collections and veneered bedroom sets.

Furniture represents permanence, forever. Furniture is a gravestone, marking the life and death of its owner. It's the squares and rectangles that contain things we hold on to, what's left behind after the heart runs dry, what burly men—pallbearers of sorts—are hired to hoist away after the funeral.

When you buy bulky furniture, aren't you making a statement? I'm settling down here and won't leave for a good long while. For this reason, I adorn my home with mostly do-it-yourself furniture: bookshelves, a dresser, a butcher-block kitchen table, four wooden chairs from K-Mart, and for my desk, a birch wooden door perched atop two file cabinets. If I need to leave it all behind, I won't experience great furniture loss.

Is it the nomad in me who's fearful, who doesn't want to be weighed down by a U-shaped couch system? After all, how could I leave it all behind and walk out the door if I had a hefty dinette set to contend with?

By the walnut dish cabinets, I told Lita about my theories of furniture. "Furniture depresses me," I said. And then I told her about my sister's green velvet pullout couch. "It's huge and funereal. When I look at it, I imagine someone lying in state, their hands gently clasped on their belly."

Lita, her head tilted to one side, asked, "How long have you had this phobia?"

"Old things scare me. Antiques. Black-and-white movies from the 30s and 40s. It's hard to watch those movies knowing all the beautiful actors and actresses are either dead or dying or senile. Though I'm not sure what that has to do with furniture."

She raised her eyebrows. I could tell she thought I was charming and quirky.

Lita plopped herself onto a leather sofa. I sat down beside her. I liked the rawhide smell. I almost felt at home with her. "I love leather couches," she said.

"Maybe I should buy this one," I said.

She put her arm around my shoulder. When a salesman walked towards us, we jumped up and left the store.

That night, on my khaki-green futon sofa, we embarked on our first kiss. It was passionate and tender and I imagined us together, resting on that expensive leather couch, clutching each other's bodies as if our lives depended on it, ten years down the line. Finally I met someone who had a career she enjoyed, who felt comfortable with her sexuality, who charmed my friends with her intellect and humor, who had just the right smells my body craved. Or was this magical connection an illusion?

I purchased my first house six months after moving to Asheville, a ranch-style home with oak floors and lots of windows. Before the owner moved out, she offered me her sofa. A huge, blue-striped cushiony sofa. On both ends were recliner chairs, similar to airplane seats—just a touch of a metal lever and you could rest as if you were in the 747 first class envoy section. I thought, Why not? Maybe a real piece of furniture would do me good. Might make me more of a real person. At the time, I didn't think twice about the pet chinchilla that wandered freely in that room, prancing on the blue shag carpet.

After taking possession of the house, I noticed the sofa's shredded, filthy arms and cushions. But the worst part was that it reeked of urine and every crevice contained pockets of chinchilla turds.

I bought a king-sized mint-green Martha Stewart cotton sheet to cover the sofa. Maybe that would make it bearable. But I knew what was underneath and I didn't want that beast near me. I called the Salvation Army, told them I had a couch I wanted to donate. Two burly sweat-stained men stepped out of a huge white truck. They walked into the chinchilla room wearing moving gloves and work boots and inspected the Beast. One of them grumbled and shook his head. He fingered the frayed armrest. "Listen Ma'am," he said. "This ain't nothing against you, but we're looking for something a little nicer." On his way out, the same man assured me that I shouldn't take it personally: "It ain't about you." Before leaving, he suggested I call Habitat for Humanity. "Maybe they'd accept it."

Was the Beast there to stay? This situation didn't help assuage my furniture phobia. How could I have been so oblivious to accept such a shabby mass of mangled couch? Perhaps I was too caught up in owning my own home to really inspect it. And the woman who offered it seemed like a reasonable person. She even left Bible quotes about love and god on the bathroom mirrors.

Later that day, two more beefy men showed up at my door. Habitat for Humanity men. Less critical of the sofa's flaws, the two men heaved the Beast up and attempted to move it out of the room. First attempt failed. They lifted it up on its side, angled it to fit through the room's entrance. But no luck. They tried every position, every angle, but the Beast wouldn't give in. It was there to stay. "They must have put this thing together in the room," one of the hefty men said. "No way it could have gotten in here otherwise." Once again, the Beast stuck its tongue out at me, like a massively obese dead person who can't fit through the door, so his family has to knock down the wall or set the house on fire. Maybe this is why I'm scared of furniture. It gets stuck in rooms. Its presence is overwhelming. And at times, big men aren't able to remove it.

I asked a handyman if he'd be able to destroy the sofa. "You name the price," I said. Two hours later, the couch was separated into bits and pieces. In fact, the two lounger seats sat on their sides, looking like airplane wreckage. I imagined the mess *was* airplane wreckage, after the bodies had been removed, before dogs sniffed for explosives.

For the first two months, Lita and I looked into each other's eyes and said this was the real thing, thank goodness we found each other. We gave each other irises and roses and pansies and cooked elaborate meals. Turkey dogs and pancakes and real maple syrup for breakfast. Apricot-laced Cornish hens for dinner. Her mother liked me. Her friends liked me. Her miniature pinscher liked me.

Still I wasn't ready to buy a dinette set.

At the time, I slept on a futon. Lita insisted I get a real bed. It wasn't that I didn't want a real bed; I just couldn't be bothered. I finally bought a mattress and boxspring when Lita arranged for a friend to help pick up a queen-sized Serta Perfect Sleeper from Sam's Club. I liked sleeping above ground level. Especially when Lita, my cure for insomnia, my promise of a lasting alliance, breathed delicately by my side.

Three months into the relationship, Lita and I lay in bed just about to drift off to sleep. Lita talked about the recording studio she intended to build in my basement.

"I'm not sure I want a recording studio in my basement," I said. "The floorboards are thin. And I'm sensitive to noise." I told her what Sherry had said about my supersonic auditory abilities, how I could hear crickets chirping in Guam.

Lita sat up. "How could we be together if you don't support my music? How could we ever live together?"

I sat up, shook my head. "This has nothing to do with your music!"

"You're still in love with Sherry, aren't you?"

I placed my hand on her hand. Lita pulled it away.

"You want to have your cake and eat it too," Lita said. "Because you're the queen. Queen Fucking Lori."

Tears welled in my eyes. I hid my face in a pillow.

Lita apologized and clutched my body, as if it were a tree branch, high above the ground.

I didn't understand Lita's accusations. Maybe she had a bad day. I started feeling around for a trap door.

Four months into the relationship, Lita and I took a trip to New York. I was excited to show her my city and bought two rolls of film to document our visit. But when we reached the East Village, my old stomping grounds, she said, "I need a drink. This city is messed up! How could you live in a place like this?"

On the morning of our first full day in Manhattan, a cold, gray, slushy day, I asked Lita if she wanted to go to the Museum of Modern Art.

"What about the Statue of Liberty?" she asked.

We made our way to Liberty Island, a place I'd never been, a place I'd never think of taking an out-of-town guest.

Accompanied by jostling throngs of tourists, we crept through the museum and learned about the statue's history and its renovation process. With the weight of my camera around my neck, we climbed the spiral staircase to the crown. Lita studied the construction of the torch, its aged copper transformed into blue. Once at the top, we looked at Lower Manhattan through the crown's windows. Lita caressed my shoulder.

For the first and only time during our trip, I put my camera's viewfinder up to my eye and snapped a photo of Lita. Visiting the Statue of Liberty was a good idea. Maybe now Lita would calm down and enjoy New York.

But on our way back to the East Village, Lita complained about overpopulation and how she couldn't wait to get back to her house in the country. "How the hell did you live here for so long?" she asked.

Lita told me to loosen up and drink more, to join a fictional support group called Party On—the antithesis to Alcoholics Anonymous. We tossed around accusations about loyalties and alcohol and commitment, and we cried and made up and cried again. And unlike the beast of a couch I had to contend with, the couch that looked so inviting to begin with, I couldn't hire a handyman to rid me of my relationship chaos. Amid the hysteria, Lita inundated me with Christmas gifts. Among them: a wok, a harmonica, a white battery-operated poodle named Hannah, a pass to the Biltmore House, an aluminum scooter, a silk shirt, a wool jacket, guitar strings. And then she told me about another present—a handcrafted bed built by her friend Sue, a woodworker. "She's only charging me for the cost of materials," Lita said.

All the gift-giving made me nervous. After all, we'd only known each other for a short time. Besides, I didn't want a handmade bed. I was happy with my mattress and box spring on the floor. And what if I didn't like the bed? Isn't furniture the kind of item—like a haircut or clothing or a dog—you should pick out for yourself? Then again, Lita assured me Sue wanted to do this for me. Would it have been rude to tell Sue to put a halt to the bed? "If you don't like it, you don't have to keep it," Lita said. "I'll put it in my house."

It took Sue four months to construct the bed, and in that time, she sent Lita blueprints and called to give updates on the work in progress. Was this bed a stand-in for a baby? The summit, the proof, the culmination of our relationship that would outlast us?

In the meantime, there were more promises and accusations and tears and knocks on my door in the middle of the night. I couldn't sleep. I couldn't eat. I crashed into parked cars. All the while, the bed loomed over me like a terrible rain cloud.

Sue drove six hours from Alabama to deliver my bed. She was proud of her work and had every reason to be. For an afternoon, she drilled and hammered and spun wing nuts and snapped dovetail corners into place, and like magic, in my room sat a beautiful bed, its headboard of delicate wood strips. She asked Lita and me to pose for a picture on the bed. And we smiled and held each other's hands and pretended all was well. Snap. For a split second, all was well.

Yet all wasn't well. Two weeks later, nine months into our relationship, I called it quits with Lita. Sue phoned to offer her condolences.

And so I am left with a bed, a bed I never asked for. I've grown to like my bed, the only substantial piece of furniture I own. And every night I lie in state, honoring what Lita and I wanted so much—the end of a long string of sad and painful departures. I see this bed as a grave marker of sorts: *Here lies the promise of what could have been, a permanent love, the love I've been waiting for, the love that'll fall into place and stay, after death and beyond.*

22

Transitions

During a discussion about the death penalty, Katie, a student in my composition class, opened a bag of Doritos and munched away. I tried to ignore her chewing and bag crackling, but soon enough I could no longer contain my anger. "This is not a cafeteria!" I said. "Put those away!"

Besides the background ventilation system blowing air from the ceiling, the room was silent. Katie sat up, glared at me and closed her bag.

Katie, a freckled-faced tomboy, arrived late on a regular basis, and after plopping herself down, she'd flip through a newspaper or read a book. When asked to participate in discussions, she'd sigh, reluctantly close her newspaper or book and stare straight ahead.

By the second week of the semester, I dreaded walking into the room.

The day the Twin Towers crumbled to the ground, Katie slumped in her desk. She said, "We deserve it. We think we're so safe. Our country is run by a bunch of assholes."

Other students shook their heads, wept, talked of relatives or friends who knew one of the victims. For the first time, students thought about war and body bags and military drafts.

Katie crossed her arms. "This is a wake-up call," she said, "to Bush and his stupid-ass cabinet." She kept at it. But now, at least, her aggression wasn't directed towards me.

During this time, I convinced myself that women were too damn difficult. My relationship with Lita was the clincher. I felt beaten down, shame that I didn't step away sooner. My crappy sense of self-worth, of thinking that's all I deserved, in addition to years of internalized homophobia, didn't help the situation. If the outside world considered LGBT folks abnormal, freaks, we start to think of ourselves as freaks. How could we truly love and respect each other if we can't respect ourselves? Maybe I wasn't really a lesbian after all.

I attempted to date men. It had been years since I'd considered dating a man, but I went out with four men over the course of ten days. Two acquaintances asked me out to dinner. One talked about sex the whole night, the other talked about wanting to sleep all day.

Then I got a phone message from a man I had met in a writing workshop six months earlier—we were both students. "I just came across a story you wrote," he told my answering machine. "It made me so happy that I thought I'd see if you wanted to have tea with me." I remembered him as a cute, lumberjack kind of guy who had written a decent story about working at an all-night diner. I called him back and we set up a date to meet. *How wonderful to find an intelligent, attractive, writer guy. And he'd probably make a wonderful father too!*

At a downtown bookshop, I found him sitting on a couch, violently flipping through the local weekly. "This paper is crap. I could read the whole thing in less than five minutes," he said. "And I'm sick of these damn Blissheads telling me to have a nice day! What if I don't want to have a nice day?" He stood up, threw the paper down, asked where I wanted to eat. Forty-five minutes later, I told him I had to grade papers. He walked me to my car and I locked the doors and drove off.

The night before the Twin Towers had fallen, Katie walked by an outdoor café where I sat with a decent guy who rambled on about his hiking expeditions. "Hi Professor," she said, sniggering to her friend, as if catching me in a lie. Fortunately, after he leaned over to kiss me in his tiny Toyota, I snapped out of that "maybe I'm not a lesbian" bubble.

On September 11th, I tried to get in touch with family and friends in New York, only to hear messages from computerized operators saying all circuits were down, to try back later. I missed my city more than ever. I missed eating breakfast at the Kiev restaurant where attentive Polish waitresses served kasha and kielbasa and huge slices of challah bread. I missed the resounding steel drums and swarming crowds in the Times Square subway station and the saxophone player who rode the subway and joked and squawked out cacophonous sounds and caused all the passengers to chuckle and chatter and then he'd say, "I'll quit playing for some spare change!"

On the night of September 11th I sat alone, over six hundred miles from Ground Zero, watching the news, while in Manhattan, single New Yorkers went to bars looking for love, or sex, with a vengeance—*crisis sex* it had been called. Broken-up couples reunited—for in a time of death and destruction, don't we all need to connect, to hold on, to find comfort in a warm body? I was a single New Yorker with no one to hold, no one to cry with. I didn't think of calling Lita. But I did think of her, how we'd find solace in one another's tears and touch and sweat, as if that would wash away the mounds of emotional debris that had already destroyed us.

A week after the attacks on New York City, I received a card from Lita: "Hope your family and friends are safe and in good spirits. Hope you're doing well too."

I stood the card on my bookshelf and thought about her laughing when I danced and chomped on a banana during my insomniac nights. "Dance that monkey dance!" she said. "Chomp, chomp, chomp on that banana."

Towards the end of our relationship, Lita had said over and over, "I miss my girlfriend." Meaning me.

"I'm the same person I was when you met me." Perhaps we were both blinded by our yearning to hold onto the perfect picture, the illusion we had imagined each other to be, the picture we clung to long after the emulsion dissolved.

Katie became more disruptive in class. Or she just stared off in the distance. I asked to speak with her in my office. "You're obviously smart," I said, "but you seem to have an attitude problem."

Katie looked at the ground and jiggled her leg. "I shouldn't be in school. I hate all of my classes." She fingered a fresh bruise, one of many, on her arm.

"Were you in an accident?" I asked.

"They're from the Fight Club," she said.

Based on the movie, Katie started the club for girls on campus, an exclusive group that took on new members by invitation only. On a weekly basis they'd get together and, two at a time, beat the crap out of each other. Katie mentioned that two other students in my class, Rachel and Cindy, girly-girls who dressed in skirts and heels, were also members of the club.

The idea of a women's fight club sounded subversive, edgy, maybe even feminist. I imagined the young women hopping around each other, swinging arms and fists, hands blocking faces, one woman pinning another's arms to the ground, a group on the sidelines cheering.

I wanted to know more. Before I could rifle off questions, she said, "I've already told you too much. First rule of the Fight Club is not to talk about the Fight Club." From her binder, she pulled a graded paper, asked why I gave her a B on it.

I looked it over, said, "First off, you moved from one topic to the next without using transitions."

"I don't believe in transitions," she said.

"But you need transitions!"

"Why?"

"I'm all for experimenting with language," I said, "but you've got to show me you know the rules before you break them."

Katie, the valedictorian of her high school class, told me she'd always gotten As on her papers. "The only thing keeping me here," she said, "is the Fight Club." She looked at her arms again. "And with the financial aid I'm getting, I can't afford *not* to be in school."

"Perhaps you could write about the Fight Club," I said, "for your next paper."

Katie shook her head. "No way. It's a private matter," she said, and stormed out of my office.

In my freshman year of college, Vicki, a tai chi expert who lived on my hall, showed women how to spar, how to strengthen our stance, how we needed to use footwork or faking to bring our partner closer to us, how to pin our opponent down if the opportunity arose. The stoned hippie boys who lived at the end of the hall watched us get sweaty, laugh, fall atop each other.

I went to a college where same-sex couples walked hand in hand, but me, I was straight. Except one day in my dorm room when I listened to Fleetwood Mac's *Rumors* over and over again while staring at the back cover of the album, at Stevie Nicks in her silk gown. I felt a pang of lust, attraction. I felt dirty. Freakish. I lifted the phonograph's arm and switched records. I put on Bob Seger's *Night Moves*. And I sat on my bed, rocking back and forth, saying to myself, "I'm not like that. I'm not like that."

To prove I was desirable, that I wasn't like "that," I drank and drank and drank and made out with boys, some of whom I didn't even like, but with a little alcohol, they became cute enough. Wasn't that what girls were supposed to do? To feel desirable? I liked the power, the attention, as if I performed magic on them, a spell of sorts, but then I left them spellbound and ran away.

During my first year of teaching college composition, the Twin Towers were two invincible rectangles hovering above lower Manhattan. Back then we were fearful, not of terrorists, but of AIDS. In class my students read and discussed *The Normal Heart*, a play that addresses love, homophobia, and the AIDS epidemic in its first years. Some students questioned why people were gay in the first place. One said, "It's *not* normal!" Others said they had relatives who were gay, that they were nice people, but they didn't want to see them expressing themselves in public. Another student, a Russian immigrant, shook her head and said, "It's their business what they do in the bed!" When I asked how they'd feel if they knew one of their teachers were gay or lesbian, one female student raised her hand and said, "I'd feel weird when she looked at me."

President Bush told us to shop, Walmart sold out of American flags, and Katie continued to undermine my authority. She tapped her fingers on her desk, grunted answers out when called upon, and sometimes fell asleep. Towards the end of the semester, students spoke about their upcoming paper topics—I had asked them to write about a current news event from a sociological perspective. Katie planned to write about a Brazilian tribe in the Amazon rainforest known for walking around in the nude, from the point of view of eighteenth-century philosopher Thomas Aquinas.

"But that's not a current event," one of the students said.

"They're still walking around in the nude, so they're current," Katie said.

No matter how much I talked to Katie outside of class, no matter how much I acted like I was in control, inside I was falling apart. Similar to my relationship with Lita, once I showed my vulnerabilities, it was hard to regain composure, not until I walked away. But when you're teaching college, you can't walk away. You're stuck for a full fifteen weeks.

After all, I'm just as vulnerable as the next person. I cry at the movies. Dumb movies. Smart movies. I can't hold back. I tell myself, *Stop crying! It's just a stupid movie! Hugh Grant would never get together with his plant-sitter.* But I can't stop. I even cry when I hear the piña colada song.

So how could I *not* get upset when I read Katie's comments about the class? Teacher evaluations are anonymous, but I knew it was Katie who wrote, "I wanted to be a writer but she totally discouraged me. She took my confidence away. Now I no longer want to be a writer. I hate her."

I questioned myself, my teaching.

Soon after the class ended, a university staff person found bloodstains on the floor of a room the group had secretly met in. The Fight Club disbanded. Katie dropped out of school.

Two years later, Katie reappeared in my poetry class, sitting in the back of the room. As if an ex-lover came back to haunt me, I wanted to run. Although she took notes and barely looked up, I stuttered when calling out names, when going over the syllabus.

But this time around, Katie behaved, made intelligent comments, wrote A papers. Midway through the semester, she stepped into my office, her eyes to the ground. She asked if I could talk with her about her midterm paper. "Have a seat," I said.

Even though we didn't acknowledge our past, its presence made itself known, like a boulder in the corner of a dream.

Together we brainstormed; she scribbled in her notebook, asked questions, and while staring at the floor, thanked me for my time.

"I hope I was helpful," I said.

She nodded her head, cowered away.

The next year, she was in another class of mine, a writing workshop. Once again her performance was stellar. During a one-on-one conference, I looked over a draft of her personal essay—a coming out story.

"It's powerful," I said, "without being sentimental. And you use transitions well."

She furrowed her brow, said, "Really?"

In her last semester, Katie asked me to be her thesis advisor. Just before graduation, during an intermission at a local music hall, Katie strolled up to me and acted as if we'd been long lost friends. "Hey, Lori," she said. "How's it going?" She introduced me to her girlfriend. I introduced her to my friend. "This is Katie," I said. "She's a student of mine, a great writer. But when she was in my composition class, she was *such* an asshole!"

Katie scowled, shut her eyes, shook her head. "I figured you'd forgotten about that."

"How could I forget?"

"I was drinking too much," she said, "and doing drugs. I *was* an asshole. I'm sorry." The musicians came back on stage and the crowd cheered.

We returned to our seats.

She attended a literary reading I participated in. Now she was my groupie in the front row.

Two years later, Katie e-mailed me with a request for a graduate school recommendation. I told her I'd be happy to write one. In a postscript, I asked about the Fight Club.

This time, in an e-mail, she obliged:

> The whole thing was very sexually charged, which I wouldn't have admitted at the time. I think it partially arose from all of these mutual and bizarre crushes my friends had on each other. I remember being in a dorm room with Cindy and another freshman and they were talking about what they called "girl crushes." I had this realization then that lesbians weren't all stereotypes and could actually be attractive and fashionable and human! And that sort of changed my life. The fight club was like making out with our fists.
>
> We used to drink 40s of High Life and sneak into this room no one ever used that had industrial carpet and this bizarre inferno theme and beat the shit out of each other (although, admittedly, most of our wounds came from rug burn when this 200-pound girl rubbed our faces in the carpet). It was pretty clear who was good and who wasn't. I think we

used to stick to sort of informal and unspoken classifications. Cindy and I were both well matched and two of the better fighters. Seems like neither one of us was willing to admit defeat so our fights would go on forever and end when everyone else got sick of watching us. We tried to leave it all in the room, you know—to get over any ego or disappointments and hug each other when it was over.

I feel lucky to have met all of those girls when it felt like everyone around us was trying to fit into the imaginary "college girl" mold. That year was filled with drunken mischief. At the end of the year about two dozen of us, boys and girls, played naked soccer on the quad in the middle of the night and walked back in the dorm barefoot, dirty, and completely undressed. Too bad everyone had to grow up.

After I sent out the recommendation, she sent me an e-mail: "Thanks again for your help. My eighteen-year-old self would never have believed that I would want your recommendation six years later."

I think about my eighteen-year-old self, drunk and slurry on White Russians, making out with boys or, sweaty and giddy, sparring with women on my dorm room floor. Who knew I'd become a college professor, wrestling metaphorically with students, teaching about the need for transitions, all the while stumbling upon a few of my own.

23
Slim-Fast Vacation

Now that I had discovered the magical world of Internet dating—an endless catalog of intrigue and possible romance—I wouldn't have to limit myself to the tiny pool of potential partners in my small Southern city. Two years had gone by since my relationship with Lita ended, since I last kissed anyone. Not for lack of trying. I went on plenty of dates—one woman told me her ex-girlfriend had accused her of strangulation but, in her defense, she said, "There weren't even any marks on her neck!" When I asked how she trained her four well-behaved Jack Russell dogs, she said, "I beat the shit out of them!" Another who, when I told her I was Jewish, said, "I once met a woman from Germany." Another was a cowgirl line-dance champion from Tennessee. One woman claimed President Bush was a feminist because he helped free Afghani women, one had been stolen as an infant and reunited with her real mother at seventeen, two had never been with women, one dressed in Goth attire and wore a dog collar, one became a good friend, one produced electronic music and, during our coffee date, told me she had eaten her dead grandmother's ashes. No one interested me.

And then I met Josie, a quick-witted Montessori teacher from Charlotte. Together we commiserated about our bad luck at Internet dating. She had just been dumped by a woman she called "Butchie."

"Why did she dump you?" I asked over e-mail. She wrote, "ALL BUTCHIE WOULD SAY WAS THAT IT WAS A FEELING. SHE COULDN'T PUT HER FINGER ON IT." Every e-mail she sent was in capital letters. I asked her why she "screamed" all the time. "I'M NOT SCREAMING. THIS IS WHO I AM."

Along with her quick wit came inappropriate sex talk and that made me nervous. Not that I'm a prude, but I always figured that people who go over the top when it comes to sex talk, especially with strangers, are the ones who have the most hang-ups in real life. I told her this. In response, she wrote, "I TALK THE TALK BUT I ALSO WALK THE WALK." I reevaluated what I wanted from her. I'd never had casual sex, not with a woman, but maybe, just maybe, I should try it. After all, it had been two years, and she did live out of town, and why shouldn't I have a little fun? So I invited Josie for a visit. Her response, "I WENT OUT AND BOUGHT ALL THESE SLINKY CLOTHES TO WEAR WHEN I'M VISITING YOU."

Josie drove two hours to my house, skidded into my driveway, and stepped out of a beat-up Pontiac. Unlike most women I met on the computer, she was a lot cuter than in her photos, sporting a short bob haircut, white sailor top, and on her feet, big black rubber-soled Mary Janes. Along with a suitcase, she carried a case of Slim-Fast through my door. It took her several minutes to jam the twelve cans into my refrigerator. Especially with a big box of donuts in the way. I had just bought a dozen Krispy Kreme donuts. "What's up with the donuts?" she asked.

"I'm on the donut diet," I said. "I'm trying to eat two or three donuts a day to gain weight."

She rolled her eyes. "Lucky you," she said. "I wish I could be on the friggin' donut diet."

We went out to dinner and she told me about Butchie. "She's having a party next week," she said. "She invited me. Then dumped me. I still might go."

"Why would you *want* to go?" I asked.

"She wasn't as cute as you," she said. "I knew we'd be friends. You and me. We're both crazy and paranoid and insecure."

"Good thing," I said, "we have a lot in common."

Back at my house, I stirred up a mix of scotch, ginger ale, and lemonade. She sipped her drink and said, "Why are you serving me something that tastes like Band-Aids?"

"What's wrong with Band-Aids?"

She tasted her drink again. "You've got a point."

On my sofa, we talked about music and art and movies and she repositioned herself so she'd be closer to me. She impressed me with her in-depth knowledge of Modernist painters and writers, including Virginia Woolf, James Joyce, and Gertrude Stein.

But she didn't make a move, and I was scared and it was getting late so I finally led her to my guest room where I sat next to her on the bed, and I thought, *It's now or never*. So I put my hand on her shoulder. She froze up. "What are you doing?" she asked.

I pulled my hand away. "I'm sorry!" I got up to leave the room.

"I didn't expect this," she said. "I didn't think you liked me."

"Forget it happened," I said.

She crossed her arms. "I don't know how to respond. I had no idea you liked me."

Humiliated and puzzled, I walked from the guest room to my bedroom. So much for a fun-filled weekend of casual sex. Before crawling into bed, I locked my door like I always did, since I was a woman living alone.

The next morning we went to a diner down the road, full of deer heads and Hollywood photos of Greta Garbo and Rock Hudson. A group of men at the next table talked about a gun show at the local convention center. Josie, in a tight white halter top, sat close to me. She told me about her father, now in a wheelchair, who abused her as a child. "The fucker fucked me up bad," she said. Her dark eyes, now sad and glassy, affixed themselves to a deer head.

"I'm sorry," I said, barely able to swallow my scrambled eggs. In the form of deep worry marks on her face and ripped up cuticles, the heaviness of this knowledge became apparent.

She sighed. "And then I had to help my mother take care of him," she said, her eyes still stuck on the deer, "after his stroke."

I put my hand on her arm. She reached for my hand, placed hers atop mine, leaned into me and whispered, "So when are you going to kiss me?"

I swallowed my egg, raised my eyebrows. Not the smoothest segue.

"I want you to do things to me," she said. "I tried to come into your room last night, but the door was locked."

After breakfast, I led her back to my bedroom and onto my bed. We kissed for a moment, but she sprang up and yelled, "You need to close the blinds! Make the room dark!"

I closed the blinds, now a tad concerned by her frantic orders.

"I need darkness!" she said.

We continued to kiss and that was okay, until I felt sweaty and asked if she wanted to take her shirt off.

"I need material!" she said. "Material between us!"

I lifted my head. "What's up with needing material?"

"Cloth," she said. "Material!"

"I know what material is," I said. "But why?"

"Haven't you been with anyone," she said, "who has intimacy issues?"

Even in the dark, I noticed her eyes, now focused on the ceiling. They started to water.

"I've got issues," she eked out.

For a while we held each other. I caressed her arm, combed my fingers through her bob, wiped a tear from her cheek. And then, as if a shrill alarm clock went off, she said, "Doesn't your dog have to go on a walk?"

We drove up to the Blue Ridge Parkway and found a short trail to hike. At one point, Josie stopped in the middle and asked me to kiss her.

"Here?" I said.

She said, "Don't you think it's sexy to kiss in public?"

I kept walking.

On the drive back to my house, we sang along to R.E.M.'s "Shiny Happy People" and stopped off at a lake where we watched my dog fetch a stick and bring it back, over and over. Josie applauded each time. I imagined her at her job, encouraging young children, affirming them with gold stars, big smiles, and loud claps.

Soon after, she packed up her Slim-Fast cans, every one of them, and drove away. Two hours later, when she got home, she e-mailed me, "I MISS YOU FEROCIOUSLY AND LONG TO HAVE SEX WITH YOU."

My magical world of Internet dating, of casual sex, was a bust. It'd been a long day. I hadn't eaten much since breakfast and now craved a donut. But when I opened the box, it was empty. The whole dozen, gone. All that remained were crumbs.

24

Unloading Bones

In the twelve years I lived in Manhattan, I was never robbed, mugged, or molested. When walking back to my Lower East Side apartment at night, I raised my shoulders and walked fast, and if I had the slightest inkling of malice directed my way, I returned a "don't-even-think-about-it" look and became a humped-back cat ready for attack.

One night as I walked home from a party on Avenue C, a man shouted from down the block, asking for the time.

"About 1:30," I yelled.

Walking towards me, he crossed over to my side of the street and asked again.

"It's 1:30," I said. Now I crossed over to the other side. I was two blocks from my apartment. A little voice in the back of my head told me to run. As fast as possible. The man chased me, but I outran him and unlocked my door and slammed it shut. Instead of feeling scared, I felt high off the rush of eluding danger, of outsmarting a thug. No one was going to chase me out of my city, my mother's birthplace, the city where my immigrant great-grandfather ran a shoe shop on Orchard Street, the city I felt proud to call home. The city whose streets and people I photographed often, sometimes slyly shooting from the hip. One autumn day I walked around the meat market district by Little West Twelfth Street and took photos of a bulldozer dropping hundreds of pounds of bones into a dumpster. The driver of the bulldozer laughed when he saw me snapping photographs: "What are ya', nuts? Whaddya takin' pictures of these bones for?"

"I've never seen so many," I said, "piled together."

"It ain't a pretty sight. But hey, whatever floats your boat."

At thirteen, I visited the World Trade Center towers, and with my twenty-five-dollar Super 8 movie camera, I captured a parachutist descending after he leapt from the roof of Tower One. I just happened to be there, visiting the new buildings with my family. And I was the only one in all of New York City to capture him on film. I ended up selling the film to NBC for a hundred bucks, and they put it on the news and displayed my name across the TV screen: "Courtesy of Lori Horvitz."

As if New York were a dysfunctional family member, I felt free to complain about Manhattan's noise and crowds, but I took offense if a non–New Yorker made a disparaging remark. During journeys backpacking in Europe, fellow travelers asked me if New York was as dirty or dangerous as it appeared on television.

"I feel safer walking in New York at two in the morning than in any other city," I said. "People are always around. They watch out."

And if people weren't around, that voice in the back of my head protected me when danger lurked, advising me to switch subway cars, walk in an opposite direction, run for my life.

On the other hand, when it comes to the heart, I've quashed instincts about soon-to-be lovers. Even if my intuition screamed, *Don't do it! You're stepping on a train heading for a brick wall!* I justified my actions: at least it'll be a fun ride. A joyride of sorts. My encounter with Josie proved just that. Maybe I needed to be a little more discerning.

In the meantime, now that I could provide a stable home for a dog, I searched for a different kind of companion: a puppy. I went to the local animal shelter, another shelter in the next county, and two different Animal Compassion Network adoption fairs. But I couldn't find the right dog, a dog I could connect with. Once again, my friends told me I was too picky. I learned that, like Internet dating, one could go to the local Humane Society website and see pictures of the puppies up for adoption. Finally I saw a border collie mix that caught my eye. I rushed off to meet her. While she sucked on a blanket thread in her cage, she stared up at me from the corner of her eye and wouldn't stop staring. She was eight weeks old and fit in the palm of my hand. My gut said go for it. I named her Isabel. Because she had the looks and markings of a full-bred border collie, I believed she was a full-bred border collie. As time passed, her body grew long and stout but her legs stayed short. My vet speculates Isabel is part corgi. She's a quirky-looking dog, stunning nonetheless. She helps ground me, at home, in nature. Each day we go for a walk in the woods, where she chases squirrels and rabbits and chipmunks. She's not fast enough to catch any of her targets, yet she keeps on trying.

In response to my personal ad with the heading "Seeking Quirky, Intelligent *Woman*," I received an e-mail. From a man, Simon: "So am I. It seems like we have a lot in common. Do you only date women?"

I had to give him credit. "I'm open to men but not actively seeking one."

He apologized for asking. "I just moved here and it would be great to find someone to show me around town."

We exchanged flirty e-mails about our lives and our families and our failed romances, and we met, and he was attractive in a blonde, boyish, Brad Pitt kind of way, albeit with extra bushy eyebrows. We had dinner and he knew how to listen and joke, and the next day we played Frisbee and drank beer and he burned Jonathan Richman and R.E.M. compact discs for me. In his arms he cradled Isabel and he said, "She's a mixture between a border collie and an inchworm!"

Yet this was not a *Chasing Amy* story where the lesbian falls for the good guy. I'm sure it happens now and again. But we remained friends. Good friends. And we talked about our dating prospects and love and literature and music, and almost two years after Lita and I broke up, he dragged me out to a bar. Julia, a woman from Memphis who I met at a party the month before, sidled up to me. She worked as a postal carrier. She told me about her girlfriend of almost four years who started sleeping with someone else.

"I kicked her out of our apartment," she said, stroking her shoulder-length blonde hair. "She sleeps with someone else and accuses me of breaking up with her!"

Before leaving, she asked for my e-mail address. I reluctantly gave it to her.

"She's cute," Simon commented. "You should go out with her."

"She's too desperate," I said. "Besides, she just broke up with her girlfriend!"

"She's nice! Go out with The Mailman!"

The next day Julia e-mailed me. We began to write long, involved letters about our lives, and, despite the fact I said I wasn't interested, I kept writing. I looked forward to her daily e-mails. Then she wrote, "I have a huge crush on you. If you're not interested, that's okay. I still want to be your friend."

I wrote, "I'm flattered, but I don't feel the same way. We'll be friends, okay?"

Four weeks later, I invited her to my house, and we played guitar and sang for each other and I showed her my poetry and we went out for Mexican food and saw a blues band. Nine hours later, before she left, I said, "We're on overtime now, aren't we?"

Maybe it was her love of documenting life—she always carried a camera with her, maybe it was the way she laughed, maybe it was the gratitude journal she kept, maybe it was the way she sang "We're on Our Way Home," maybe it was the way she held her kitten in the crook of her elbow that brought out a beauty I hadn't seen earlier. And my gut said, *Yeah, go for it.* Just like that parachutist who in 1975 worked his way up to the top of Tower One, jumped off, and descended towards safety.

Julia and I stayed together for two and a half years. During that time, we took lots of walks on the Blue Ridge Parkway with my dog and her decrepit springer spaniel, Wendell. Isabel liked to jump on Wendell, tried to play with him, but he had no interest in playing, only scavenging the roads for leftovers.

I learned that Julia was a homebody. I liked to go out. She got up at the crack of dawn. I liked to sleep in. She said I was overanalytical and at the movies, she suggested that I sit back and enjoy the films, not critique them. She liked to have music on all the time. I at times enjoyed silence. She liked to invite crowds along if we went out (the more the merrier), I liked to spend time in small groups and engage in intimate conversation. We went to therapy. We split up. We got back together. Until we split up for good. We tried. Now we remain friends. She introduces me as "the best ex-girlfriend."

Six months after we had met, Julia and I walked the streets of Lower Manhattan, taking in the sun, visiting art galleries, eating at my favorite Indian restaurant, Taj Mahal. She wanted to know all about me, my city. We walked along East Seventh Street and I pointed out a top-floor apartment above a Polish travel agency. "That's where I lived for five years. A sixth-floor walk-up."

Her eyes, one brown, one blue, reflected the sun. "Bet your legs got strong," she said.

I asked her to pose in front of the travel agency and took her picture.

The next day we visited Ground Zero, a field of craters enclosed in fencing and ripped tarp. We both stood in silence, watching trucks haul objects from one spot to another. Julia pointed out rusted beams in the shape of a crucifix. Tourists posed in front of the site and snapped away, but I had no desire to document this tragic scene. Why would anyone take pictures of what they don't want to remember?

We studied an embossed list of the dead. I saw a name I recognized. A girl in my sixth-grade class. It didn't seem all that long ago when Mr. Diamond, our teacher, spoke about the women's liberation movement and played Helen Reddy's "I am Woman." I remember Deborah mouthing along with the words: "I am strong, I am invincible, I am woman!"

I looked again at the cratered area in front of me and shook my head. I imagined the thousands of New Yorkers, numbed, shuffling home in silence on September 11th, as if someone turned the volume of the city all the way down.

I told Julia the story of the parachutist, how I had been the only one to capture him on film. "And NBC News aired it twice."

"That's impressive. Famous at thirteen!"

Maybe this is how love works. Maybe you can't look for it. Maybe you just have to be in the right place at the right time. And like magic, it'll drift towards you. When you least expect it.

Julia and I walked to Battery Park and stared out across the Hudson, past the Statue of Liberty, towards New Jersey. A couple passed by and Julia asked if they'd take our photo. She handed over her camera. "Try to get the Statue of Liberty in the picture," she said. We put our arms around each other, smiled, and heard the camera's click.

Tourists lined up for the boat to Ellis Island, where so many immigrants, including my great-grandparents, began a new life. Julia touched my shoulder. "Thanks for showing me around," she said.

25

Father's Advice

During each conversation I have with my father, he insists I go to the local synagogue. He repeats himself over and over. "The rabbi is very nice," he says. "It'll do you good."

But I'm not one for organized religion.

When I moved to North Carolina for my teaching job, I left New York, but New York didn't leave me. Now I was a New Yorker in the South. More of a New Yorker than ever before. I'm a Yankee Jew in a place where most people can count their Jewish friends on one hand. I'm a novelty. After learning I'm Jewish, people here are awed. Some ask if I'm one hundred percent Jewish.

"Full-blooded," I say.

"Wow. That's so cool!"

Although I'm a non-practicing Jew, I have begun to embrace my heritage. I even taught a college course, Art of the Holocaust. In class, we looked at all forms of art, some created during the Third Reich, some made later as a result of it. I told my class the enormity of the Holocaust, the reality of it, didn't hit me until I walked through Auschwitz. One student confided in me that his family is German Jewish. Even though most of his family got out in time, he said, "They never discuss the Holocaust. I'm glad I'm finally learning about it." The material we read and watched and listened to was difficult and disturbing, and by mid-semester we were numbed by the atrocities. Yet at the end of the semester, most students agreed that despite the emotionally taxing material, they were glad they had taken the class. And little did they know, much of the material was new to me. One student comment from a course evaluation: "Since our professor is Jewish, she really knows what she is talking about."

The last time my father visited, I interviewed him with my video camera. Usually he talks fast, repeats himself, stutters, interrupts. To have a conversation with him is next to impossible. A majority of the time, he fixates on two topics: Judaism and Israel.

But on camera he sat up straight and spoke slowly. My father, the son of a rabbi, talked about the anti-Semitism he experienced as a child growing up in the Midwest. "Our neighbors were surprised we didn't have horns," he said.

I asked him what his favorite college course was.

"Cafeteria," he said.

"Didn't you have a favorite class?"

"No," he said. "I liked to sit in the cafeteria and read the newspaper."

After college, my father accepted a job selling children's clothing in the Midwest. But he got fired and became a middle-school history teacher.

Since my mother died, I've tried to understand my father. Tried to find compassion for a man who drove the car in which his wife of thirty-two years was killed. To understand why he always insisted I take the easy way out: "Just give your class standardized tests! Use the Scantron." To understand why, when I got accepted into a PhD program, he said, "Just get a job in an advertising agency and stop with the school already." To understand why, when I showed him a glowing write-up about my teaching, he said, "Who wrote this? This is beautifully written! Where did this woman go to school?"

Why was it so hard for him to dole out a few scraps of support? Was he too frustrated with his own life? Is that why he chose to discourage me from going to grad school and encouraged me to settle for a career I wouldn't be happy with?

I try to find compassion for this man who, when I was a teenager, constantly badgered me about why I didn't have any friends. This man who, for years after Sunshine, my white pocket poodle, disappeared in the middle of a snowy college campus, asked, "Where's the white pup?"

During the interview, my father spoke about the terrible fights his parents had when he was a child.

"And what did you do when they fought?" I asked.

He looked straight into the camera and said, "I sat in the closet and read the dictionary."

Now my father is a white-haired, hunched-over man. He talks about his rotting teeth, his bad back, the possible connections between his ailments and Lou Gehrig's disease.

I know he's trying his best. I know he's proud of me. His girlfriend told me so.

At the end of the interview, I asked my father to read a poem aloud, a poem I had written about him, composed of his own statements:

Father's Advice

You're too lonely, that's why you can't sleep at night.

You're out of touch with the world.

You need to watch television.

Why don't you join a synagogue?

Why are you always running off to Europe?

What are you running away from?

Why don't you visit Epcot Village, you'd love it.

You don't need to run around Mexico shitting all day long.

Get out of your room and stop pulling on yourself.

Run around the block a few times.

Of course you have cavities, you eat candy from morning 'til
   night.

Invite a friend when you drive a long ways.

You need someone to talk to.

Ask the man if there's enough oil in the car.

Don't let anyone in the car. If you crash, they'll sue the *kishkas*
out of you.

Why don't you become a speech pathologist?

It's good money and you don't have to work too hard.

You should be making eighty thousand dollars a year by now—
just get a job in a bank, join the army, take the postal clerk
test, become a psychiatric nurse, open up a Carvel.

You don't need to be reading Marx.

He was a filthy bastard who never took a bath.

Don't work too hard on your papers for school,

Just copy from the book and write *Ibid*.

When are you going to finish your degree already?

Just write three odes and call it a day.

Better yet, write something like Beowulf,

People will think you're a genius.

Send Grandma a recent photo of yourself.

She wants to set you up with a police sergeant.

He's Jewish. Why don't you find someone already?

Get married and get it over with.

When he finished reading the poem, he smiled, made a goofy
face.

"Were you responsible," I asked, "for saying those words?"

"I can't deny I have said similar things," he said, broken up by
laughter.

I laughed too.

26

The Golden Cord

Six hundred miles from my home in North Carolina, while at an art colony just north of Chicago, I strolled through virgin prairie and wept. My dog, Isabel, had disappeared from a friend's farm. My friend had put up flyers, posted pictures on lost-animal websites, checked in with the local shelters, and searched every crevice of her land. Another friend phoned the sanitation department to find out if they had disposed of any dead dogs. My sister in New York said, "I hope she wasn't eaten by coyotes." Another friend went to my house to put out food and water on my porch on the off chance that Isabel might find her way back. Yet another suggested I get in touch with an animal psychic.

I couldn't write. I couldn't sleep. Although I was skeptical about animal psychics, I was willing to try anything. I phoned one psychic, but she was at her day job at an electrical supply company and couldn't talk long. She said Isabel hurt her right paw. "I know she's out there," she whispered. "She might have lost her way." The psychic suggested I call for Isabel three times and tell her I'd be back soon, that she needed to make her way back to the farm. "You need to pray for her every chance you can," she added.

I had minimal experience with prayer and psychics. In fourth grade, before my clarinet solo in front of the band teacher, I chanted a Hebrew prayer to make it into junior varsity band. I got in. When I was a graduate student, I paid a visit to a psychic, mainly out of boredom. In her sixties, the psychic wore a Cleopatra wig, which she adjusted from time to time. "Honey," she said. "You need to do something with your hair." She mentioned an Italian man in my life. It was true I once had an Italian-American boyfriend, but I hadn't kissed a man in years. She asked for the birthdates of my parents and proceeded to go into a deep trance. When she came out, she looked straight at me, and with conviction, said, "Your mother hates your father. You must have had a difficult childhood."

I didn't tell the psychic my mother was dead. My parents had quarreled often, and on occasion threatened divorce.

The day after I met with the Cleopatra psychic, I went to lunch with a journalist friend. When I told her the psychic's name, she said, "I know her. The police hire her to find dead bodies."

Now, before going back in the prairies, I phoned another animal psychic, but she was booked up for the next week. She gave me the e-mail address of yet another psychic. So I sent off an e-mail, and walked and wept and pleaded for my dog to come home. *Please Isabel, please come back to the farm. I love you. Please come back. I'll be home soon.*

Another resident at the art colony, a Brazilian sculptor, noticed my teary face when she strolled by. "She's just being a dog," she said. "She'll come back." In an effort to change the subject, she praised the essay I had read aloud the night before, a story about a relationship I had with another woman. Although this was a group of artists, all liberal thinkers, I felt nervous about reading the story, about exposing myself like that. During our dinners, fellow colonists talked about husbands and boyfriends and failed marriages. But I plowed ahead with my lesbian story. Even in this environment, it felt risky to come out, to talk specifics. But when I did, walls broke down.

Soon after, one of the colonists asked to speak with me about her "confused" stepdaughter. Now I was the expert on lesbians.

In the middle of the prairies, the Brazilian sculptor asked, "How could you ever really define your sexuality?" She had a husband and six-year-old boy. Together we walked back to her studio, where I showed her a lesbian dating website. Six months before, I had put a profile on the site, including a picture of myself holding Isabel. In the photo, with her ears pointed out and recent haircut, she looked like a koala bear.

"In the last six months," I told her, "I've met lots of women through the site. Some have become good friends." I neglected to mention that during this time, I'd had three flings with Internet women. Besides an aborted attempt at a fling with Josie, I always looked at women as sacred ground, always spent time getting to know potential girlfriends.

Internet Date Number One, a pediatrician from Richmond, Virginia, had an undergraduate degree in literature, read all the Russian classics while in medical school. She was tall and thin and blonde. Brilliant. Sexy. Had a career she loved. But there were catches. She liked to drink. A lot. She admitted to being "slightly narcissistic." And she didn't eat much because she "liked feeling hungry."

"So did Karen Carpenter," I said.

In response, she gave a medical explanation of how Karen Carpenter's body had gone into shock and why that wouldn't happen to her.

But it wasn't the eating and drinking issues that made me wince. It was that she'd been with lots and lots of men and only one woman, a woman she was in love with, a married woman with children who had no intention of leaving her husband. Although the doctor implied that the affair was over, now they were only friends, they continued to have an illicit affair. I disregarded this knowledge for the attention the doctor showered upon me. She e-mailed me constantly and text messaged little memos like, "Just to let you know, I have a pierced navel. If you're into that sort of thing."

I told a friend about the pediatrician. In response, she said, "She's presenting you with a bouquet of red flags!"

I laughed. "And my arms are wide open."

The doctor drove six hours to visit me. She said she drank "three or four" beers while on the road. Before she arrived, I had swigged down a couple shots of Scotch. We went out to a bar and drank more. "Drink all you want," she said. "I have disposable income."

At the bar, she typed a message into her Blackberry, her thumbs flying onto the tiny keypad. When I learned she was receiving and sending text messages to the other woman, I said, "You need to put that thing away," pointing to her phone. "That's rude!"

She typed in a final message and turned the phone off. "I want you to kiss me," she said.

We sat in a crowded, trendy downtown bar. "My students might see!"

She ordered more drinks, and when I said I'd had enough, that I didn't want to get a DUI, she said, "Come on! You don't live that far!"

On the drive back to my house, she asked me to pull over and kiss her. I obliged. It was sexy. I was in the car with a sexy, drunk doctor.

The next morning, she said, "I think I'm a lesbian." And then her face turned dour. "I feel bad, like I cheated on her."

"I feel like I'm having a threesome," I said. "With you and your married girlfriend."

Internet Date Number Two, a medical supply representative from Chattanooga, didn't care much for her day job. Her real passion was working with her local search and rescue team. My friend listened to her phone message and commented, "She sounds like a confident, country butch." I'm not into butch women. She sent me lots of pictures of herself and her dog, a Lassie-type collie. She didn't look that butch. In fact, she looked like Hillary Clinton. She had a nice jawbone and deep, green eyes, and if I hadn't seen the photos, I wouldn't have written back. We had nothing in common.

Before we met, she asked twenty questions. One was what famous person I'd like to lunch with. I hate that question and didn't answer it. The one person she wanted to lunch with was Condoleezza Rice. I found out she voted Republican in the last election. I didn't know if I could date a Republican.

When I met her in Chattanooga, her appearance and gestures were more butch than I had imagined. She wore a cell phone and pocketknife on her belt. "Nice to meet you, Asheville," she said. She referred to the women from her last two Internet encounters as "Memphis" and "Pensacola."

She leaned forward, made a table of her back and yelled for her dog: "Come on, Mabel!" Her dog rushed up and jumped on her back, its spindle legs shaking until she gave a hand signal for the dog to jump down. "I just taught her that trick!"

Isabel, sitting between my legs, stared up at me, as if to say, "Who the fuck is this woman and her ridiculous dog?" When Mabel started sniffing Isabel, Isabel growled. Mabel growled back, and before Mabel could pounce on her, I picked Isabel up.

Ms. Search and Rescue laughed. "They're just working things out." Perhaps we were too.

I was intrigued with the passion she had for finding bodies, dead or alive. When we went out that night, she opened doors for me. I slipped into girly-girl mode. Before dessert arrived, she flipped open her cell phone and showed me a picture—a naked dead man in a pit. The man had dug a hole in the woods, laid in it, covered up the pit with a piece of slate, and overdosed on drugs.

Mabel the collie, during a search-and-rescue effort, sniffed the man out. A pair of stilettos, auburn wig, and a gold-sequined cocktail dress sat on a rock near the dead man's body. "I'm not supposed to be showing you this," she said.

I held the phone in my hand, examined the grainy picture. "What am I supposed to be seeing?" I asked.

"Look," she said. She leaned her arm against mine, pointing to the image, "That's the ditch, and that's a leg."

I looked away from the phone. "So," I said, "this is what turns you on?"

She snapped the phone shut, moved in even closer. "That's not all that turns me on."

Like a stupid girly girl, I smiled and looked away.

When I left the next morning, we still had nothing in common.

Internet Date Number Three lived in a Chicago suburb. A first generation Italian-American, she grew up one town over from me on Long Island, had a thick New York accent, short dark hair, and big brown eyes. She made a ton of money as an actuary and didn't know why her employers paid her so much, why they kept giving her raises. We had planned to meet up while I was at the art colony. During our first phone conversation, she told me she didn't put up with shit in relationships and wouldn't be in a relationship if she had to raise her voice. "I don't let anything bother me," she said. She sounded rough, hard.

"But sometimes there are misunderstandings," I said, "and having an argument is part of communicating."

"I'd rather walk away," she said. "Maybe that's why I haven't been in a relationship in eight years."

We met. We flirted. She wined and dined me and got mad when I offered to pay my share.

I told her I'd seen ghosts. "There's one in the house where I'm staying."

She said she didn't believe in things she couldn't prove.

"What about huge concepts," I said, "like life and love and death?"

I already knew things wouldn't work out. She claimed all women were catty and manipulative. Also, she liked to talk about sports cars.

"I'm going to buy a Thunderbird convertible," she said.

"Aren't they like forty thousand dollars?"

"Try sixty thousand," she said.

But I accepted an offer to come home with her. "You need to meet my dog," she said. Henry, a huge, wrinkly shar pei, yelped and cried when we got to her house, and then followed her every move. Before offering me a beer, she unwrapped four Starbucks cookies and fed them to Henry, one at a time. "Some say my relationship with Henry," she said, "is a little unhealthy."

Henry followed us into the bedroom, made himself comfortable right smack in the middle of the bed.

"You think Henry could get down," I asked, "for a little while?"

She pushed him to one side of the bed. "He's used to being up here with me."

And there I was, caught in another threesome.

Later, when she looked at me, she said, "You think too much. Stop thinking."

"If I weren't thinking, I'd be dead," I said. "What are *you* thinking about?"

"The sky is blue," she said.

"What's wrong with thinking?"

"I keep myself busy so I don't have to think."

The next night, she picked me up in her Mercedes SUV, and during and after dinner, she drank and drank and drove aggressively and screamed at other drivers, and when she stopped for a woman at a crosswalk, she leaned out of the car window and screamed, "Fucking skinny bitch! You can say 'thank you!'"

Afraid to say anything, I prayed to make it back to the retreat alive.

The day after my encounter with the aggressive driver, I learned
of Isabel's disappearance. Since then, I had called for her in the
prairies, checked in with my friend who had been watching her,
prayed for Isabel's return.

Finally the other animal psychic e-mailed me back, said she'd
been out of town. She asked me to phone her. Speaking in a thick
Brooklyn accent, she said, "I can't talk right now. I got an iguana
in the bathtub." She told me to send pictures of Isabel and the
location where she had last been seen. "I'm gonna use my pendu-
lum," she said, "and dowse over a map where your dog was lost."
We made an appointment to speak the next day, but until then,
she said, "Call for Isabel. Tell her you'll be home soon. Visualize
holding her in your arms."

That night my friend Jessica phoned. "I heard about Isabel.
I'm so sorry." She offered to go out to the farm and call for Isabel,
as a last resort.

I tried to write. But all I could do was stare at my screen-
saver, a picture I took of Isabel herding a donkey. Without her, I
couldn't imagine going home, her toys and bones and tennis balls
scattered around my house.

When I spoke to the animal psychic, Isabel had been missing for eight days. "Isabel lost her way," she told me. "She's okay.
She's hungry. She might have been taken in by a not-so-sane
man in a trailer." The psychic led me on a guided meditation
called The Golden Cord. "We gotta calm her down," she said,
"so she can think clearly about how to make her way home." She
asked me to open my heart like a window and imagine a cord
leading from my heart to Isabel's heart. She told me to imagine
Isabel finding her way back to the farm. We did this for forty-
five minutes. "Because you went on an adventure, Isabel wanted
to go on one too," she said. Before we got off the phone, she said
to keep imagining that cord, connecting my heart to Isabel's.

Thirty minutes after I got off the phone, Jessica called. "Guess
who's here with me."

"Isabel?"

"When I was driving up to the farmhouse," she said, "she was pacing back and forth in the driveway, out of breath, waiting."

I gripped the phone.

"She definitely lost weight," Jessica said. "She's dirty and has burrs all over her. She's limping on her right paw. But she's sure happy to see me. She's jumping up and crying."

That night at the residency, the colonists and I drank wine, toasted to Isabel.

And so Isabel went on her adventure; I went on mine. She got trapped in a trailer with a not-so-sane man. I got trapped, among other places, in a Mercedes SUV. Both of us got filthy and smelly and scratched up from our journeys. Perhaps we needed to venture out, for the moment, to go on a quest, to find out what was on the other side. And—maybe it was faith, maybe it was luck, maybe it was by the grace of god—we both made it back alive.

27

Into the Arms of Strangers

Penny, my girlfriend of three months, slipped on her sneakers and stared at the ground. "I don't want to be gay," she said. "Do you?"

"It's not a matter of wanting," I said, staring at the smoke detector in our Provincetown motel room.

"Well," she said, her thick Southern drawl making the word into three syllables, "I just think it's wrong." She tied her laces and plodded towards the door.

A month into our relationship I had planned this trip to Provincetown, a town where Penny, perhaps, could accept who she was, away from the clutches of Southern Baptists and Bible quotes still alive and kicking in North Carolina, where we both resided.

Outside the motel window, the Atlantic slapped the shoreline, the same ocean I had crossed time and time again when I wandered through Europe for months at a time, searching for someone to talk to, a foreigner who made me articulate who I was. My travels helped me find the confidence to break free of the shy girl I had been, the girl stuck in a hot pink Long Island bedroom. But here I was, a New York Jew, having to articulate myself to a closeted Southern Baptist.

In Europe, I rode trains and busses through Turkey, Greece, Romania, Moscow, obsessing about men, then women, then consumed by fear—fear that I might really like women, so I kept stepping onto trains, waiting on platforms for connections, having romances with foreign women. Not until I began to write, in a serious way, did I stop taking off to foreign destinations, when writing became a place where I could take risks, explore, come to terms with my sexuality.

Yet even on my own turf, I still dated foreigners.

Penny had a Southern accent I could barely understand. When she said she didn't want to be gay, I felt like I did when my German girlfriend mentioned her grandparents still had warm feelings for Hitler. I should have gotten out, I should have told Penny, *Sorry, I've already been through this. It's taken me years to accept myself and I don't want to go back to square one.* But I didn't. Maybe she'd come around. Maybe magic could happen.

Penny and I watched videos, alternating on who got to pick. I chose the first video, *Into the Arms of Strangers: Stories of the Kindertransport,* a film about an underground railroad that saved the lives of Jewish children during World War II.

And then we moved on to her pick, *The 40-Year-Old Virgin.*

During my next pick, *Borat,* Penny stopped the video after the Borat character pointed to a pickup truck and asked a car salesman if the truck would be good for running down Jews. The salesman didn't flinch.

"Why does he hate Jews?" Penny asked.

I sighed. "It's a parody," I said.

When my friend first introduced us, I thought Penny looked like Joni Mitchell, but Penny only said hello and continued to talk about an upcoming bike race with other outdoorsy women at the table. We didn't speak that night, not until I zipped up my jacket and said goodbye. That's when Penny asked me about my job and told me about hers. She worked as a PACU nurse.

"What's that?" I asked.

"Post-anesthesia care unit," she said. "I take care of patients who are waking up after surgery."

"Are most of them out of it?"

"Some are violent," she said. "I have to talk them down." She tightened the scarf around her neck.

"Sounds scary," I said.

"I manage."

On our first date, Penny hobbled towards me in tight jeans and pointy cowboy boots, her legs bowed out as if she'd been riding a horse for a week.

"You okay?" I asked.

"I ran thirty miles today."

"Thirty miles?"

"It was a run for Africa," she said. "To raise money."

We walked into the restaurant. "Thirty miles?" I said again. "I don't even like to drive thirty miles."

Penny didn't say much or eat much. She jiggled her leg and didn't make much eye contact. I asked about her stint in the military. That's where she learned to be a medic and then went on to nursing school, becoming the first college graduate in her extended family. When Penny was in junior high, her mother got together with an abusive man, so Penny's aunt took her in and brought her to church to get saved. "They don't like gay people," she said.

"I never met a gay person until college," I told Penny. "When I told my mother about him, she said, 'He's probably just pretending to be gay.'"

Penny stared at her food. After a long pause, she talked about her love of Colorado and Wyoming, where she worked as a traveling nurse. "I miss the landscape," she said. "The sky."

"Why'd you come back?" I asked.

She dipped her fork into a rice dish, her hand trembling. "To be closer to Nanny."

Her grandmother, who Penny loved more than anyone, was now bedridden. Her aunt took care of Nanny, but once every few weeks, Penny drove the four hours to South Carolina and relieved her aunt of caretaking duties for the weekend.

I mentioned an upcoming literary reading.

"A reading?" she asked.

"I write stories about stuff that happens to me," I said.

Penny didn't understand the concept of revealing personal

details to strangers. I explained that writing is an outlet for me, for making sense of life.

She took a swig of her beer. "Well," she said, "I think I get it. Like my outlet is exercise. If I don't do it, I go crazy."

"Exactly," I said.

We did have something in common. A passion. A drive. And our dogs. Penny's dog, a boxer-Chihuahua mix, all muscle with a pointy Chihuahua snout, romped with my dog, a border collie-corgi mix. The two odd-looking mutts, both the same size and weight, cried and danced when they greeted each other, as if they finally found their life partners.

On our third date, Penny and I drank beer in my kitchen. I listened to how Penny advocated for patients, how she spoke up to negligent doctors. At one point I referred to someone as "poor white trash" and she fell silent. She took offense. I apologized. I admired her for having pride in her poor Southern roots.

I walked Penny out to my driveway and we kissed for the first time.

Thirty minutes later, she drove away. And then she phoned. "Sorry about that," she said.

"What's there to be sorry for?"

"Maybe you didn't want that."

"It was really nice," I said.

A month after the Provincetown trip, Penny planned to move to Colorado. Then stay. Then go. Then stay. Then go. Even though she didn't want to be a lesbian, she wanted to spend nights with me and do things that lesbians did. We continued to watch films together. She picked *Live Free or Die Hard*.

Two months after the Provincetown trip, Penny went out with co-workers and drank beer after beer. She met a guy and gave him her number. "He wants to go mountain biking with me," she later said.

"Don't you think he wants more than that?" I asked.

"I'm not telling him I'm gay."

In spite of my reservations about Penny's reluctance to tell mountain biker guy the truth, a week later, at midnight, we watched my pick, *Annie Hall*. Just when Woody Allen visits his girlfriend's family in the Midwest and imagines her grandmother imagining him as a Hasidic Jew, Penny's phone rang. It was Mountain Biker Guy. He wanted to go out for a beer.

By dating a woman who insisted she didn't want to be a lesbian, did I really think there would be rules to abide by? Penny's aunt quoted the Bible and often went on about "the sinning homosexuals," so it made sense why Penny didn't respect herself and struggled with her sexuality. But I had my own issues to contend with. I took inventory of my dating history. For three years, I dated a Mexican who hung around with a friend who supplied her with cocaine. That same friend was in love with her and wouldn't acknowledge our relationship. How was I respecting *myself* when I continued a romance with a Spaniard who screamed at me after I wouldn't kiss her because of the big herpes sore on her lip? "You are so paranoid!" she said. "I cannot believe you!" Or finding myself in a love triangle in dictator-run Romania with my closeted lover, Rita. Even after she shattered my heart, I spent time with her as if our Romanian holiday never happened.

Like many women, I suppose, we get attached to the companionship, the intimacy, the sex. Maybe we get attached to the pain, if that's what's familiar. But we figure out a way to overlook it, to justify it. A friend of mine justified fifteen years of an unhappy marriage. She said, "You're the only one who told me not to get married, and you were right." When she had told me about her impending marriage, I asked if there was passion between her and her fiancé. "Not really," she had said. "But that's not the most important thing." During the first part of the marriage, she told me, despite the lack of passion, despite her husband's drinking, she felt so normal, so settled, so part of the mainstream. She was somebody's wife.

One night we watched Penny's movie pick, *Miss Congeniality*. "What a load of sexist crap!" I said. "Sandra Bullock had to have an extreme makeover in order to get that asshole guy?" I explained how this movie would be perfect to show to my Intro. to Women's Studies class and have students look at it through a feminist perspective.

"I'm no feminist," Penny said.

"Of course you are!"

"I'm not one of those women," she said, shaking her head, "who screams and marches through the streets."

When we let go of our differences, Penny and I shared tender moments. When she grilled swordfish for me on her porch and we held hands and watched the sunset, and she told me about her Paw-Paw who used to take her hunting, and I told her about my Grandpa Harry, a Russian immigrant, who gave me Yodels and called me his little girl but threatened to throw my poodle out the window after she peed on his carpet.

On our last night together, before she moved to Colorado, I picked out a documentary, *Forgiving Dr. Mengele*. Penny looked at the DVD cover and said, "Do we have to watch another Holocaust film?" She brought a copy of *Fried Green Tomatoes*, her favorite movie. "I must have watched this," she said, "at least fifteen times."

In the early nineties, after I had first seen the film, I argued with a straight friend about the two main characters. I insisted they were lesbians.

Now Penny and I watched the film and held each other by my fireplace. "So," I said, "is it obvious that Idgie and Ruth are lesbians?"

"I reckon."

Soon after she moved, Penny met a Dutch woman who lived in Colorado. Maybe because Penny left the South, maybe because she didn't need to interact with her aunt on a regular basis since her grandma died, but two years later, Penny legally married her girlfriend in Amsterdam. She invited me to their reception in Colorado. Although I couldn't make it, I sent them wishes for a lifetime of happiness and health. Her Facebook status: married.

My friend who had introduced us said, "I didn't mean for you guys to *date*. You had *nothing* in common." At least I had the chance to travel to Penny's part of the world, a world I hadn't seen before. Now, on the same shelf as my photo albums from Europe—photos of me and the Brit in Romania, me and the Spaniard in Paris, me and the German in France—there are photos of me and Penny in an album, one photo of us holding each other in Provincetown, cheap cowboy hats upon our heads, drinking mint juleps on the balcony of our motel room, the ocean waves slapping the Atlantic shoreline just above our shoulders.

28

Fahrenheit or Celsius: Long Distance Love in Degrees

I

You warn me of Madrid summers, the criminal heat, so before
I arrive, I ask if you have a fan; you borrow an industrial-sized
ventilador, loud as an airplane about to soar into the sky. I don't
mind the noise, but you can't sleep. You don't mind the heat,
your blood accustomed to scorching stillness, but my Russian
blood begs for a breeze. We go to Cuenca, a small village two
hours away but it's even hotter and the hotel's air conditioning is
broken. We watch a TV program, an interview with Fidel Cas-
tro at one of his mansions. In the morning, I ask the clerk about
the AC, and he says they're working on it, but you say, "All the
time it's like this in Spain. Everything is broken." And then we
visit Toledo, even hotter. Japanese tourists swarm the streets and
the hotel's AC makes our lips turn blue. "It's like this," you say. I
turn the AC off. You tell me your stomach's upset, get under the
covers, and watch a gossip program about Franco's grandchil-
dren, the volume at a deafening level.

2

A friend of yours notices we only speak in present tense.
Perhaps this is true, both of us novices at the other's language.
Present tense is easy; we don't need to think about the future or
past, only the moment, still, frozen, like a cube of ice, a confident rectangle until it dribbles and slithers and evaporates as if
it were never there, or a photograph, time frozen, but as soon as

an image is exposed to light, it begins to fade. We understand the language of light, both of us calmed by capturing images: of each other, alone, together, sometimes we use a self-timer, one of us zipping into the frame. Once, when we survey a contact sheet, you point to an image and say, "I like this one. I'm not pretty in it, but I don't like to be pretty in photos."

3

Four months after our Madrid rendezvous, we meet in record-cold Paris; you don't bring a hat or gloves, only a thin sweater, holey scarf, and a big, green coat. I lend you my gloves and hat, and we get off the Metro one stop too soon and walk to your friend's loft. Once there, we hold our frosty hands over steamy radiators. Across the street, turquoise Metros swoosh by, another stops, picks up passengers, starts up again. The constant rumbling makes you feel safe, like a heartbeat. I say, "I'll use earplugs when I sleep," but even with earplugs, there's no way to muffle the rumbling. You say, "The Metro is my friend."

4

One morning in Paris, we both wake with nightmares: on your way to the airport, you saw a car slide off a mountain and stopped to help. The driver had a bloody face but was more concerned with his appearance than his injury. After another person stopped to help, you told the injured man he'd be okay and rushed to catch your flight, a flight to see me. But you woke up en route. In my dream, I stood on a Greenwich Village rooftop and watched an airplane lose control and nosedive into Lower Manhattan. After we exchange dreams, I say, "I hope you missed your flight."

5

On New Year's Eve in Paris, your friend tells us it's best to stay indoors. He says, "On this night, many people set cars on fire."

So we drink champagne, and when the clock strikes twelve, we stick our heads out the window and scream into the frozen night. Revelers blow horns and the Metro stops and chugs on, passengers illuminated, placid in their seats, and I imagine you on one of those trains, me running to catch it, but the doors shut. Your big brown eyes stare through the window. I slap the door and the train pulls away.

6

An African man stands by his display of tiny Eiffel Tower replicas, the real Eiffel Tower hovers in the background. I ask you to pose between the replicas and the real thing and you stand, hands in pockets of your big green coat, the African man also looking my way. But only the Eiffel Tower comes out clear. Four days later, in London, we walk across the Thames on footbridge. A bitter wind slaps us from every direction. I can't look anywhere but down, until a Polish couple asks if I'd take their picture. Afterwards, I hand them my camera and we pose. I ask them to take another, but they don't understand and hand the camera back. Now we are two blurred women, a clear London Bridge in the background.

7

In Spanish, the word *tiempo* translates into *time* and *temperature*, and together, anything could happen. Like developing photographs under red safelight glow—so much depends on the temperature of the developing solution, and if one exposes the paper to too much light, it turns black, black as the basement room we inhabit in London. Exhausted and in bed, we talk of the freezing weather and, frail as a tiny sparrow, your eyes tear up and you say, "I need someone to save me." We talk of our dead mothers and a light flash appears from the corner of the room. It flashes again and I say, "Maybe it's your mother, our mothers," and you say, "No, it's from the cars outside." You pull back the curtains and a dark shade covers the entire window, no way light could seep in. You come back to bed and say you don't believe in *fantasmas*, but when I leave to use the toilet you say, "Please, please come back soon."

29

OpenWide66

On my first morning at an art colony, a poet who lived across the hall asked if I had heard someone typing in the mansion's attic above my room. "It was so loud!" she said. "All night long!"

I didn't hear the typing, but I had used a deafening fan and earplugs to block out the classical music in the distance.

"I can't believe you didn't hear it," the poet said. "It sounded like one of those old electric typewriters. The ones you can change the ball on."

"A Selectric?" I said.

"Why would anyone," she asked, "want to work up there?" She heard classical music too, also coming from the attic. After we finished our coffee, we opened the door to the attic and walked up the creaky steps. Crammed with old costumes spilling from big trunks, antique furniture, paintings, and yellow-haired porcelain dolls with lifelike eyes, it would have been impossible for anyone to work up there. At the top of the steps, a red Selectric typewriter sat on the floor, its unplugged cord a wiggly snake. A few feet away, a dusty record player rested atop a trunk, Beethoven's "Symphony no. 3 in E Flat" cued up on its turntable.

At dinner, a painter said she'd been to the colony twenty times before and knew each room intimately. When I told her the name of my room, her eyes looked downward, her face immobile. "Oh," she said, then stuck her fork into a chicken cutlet.

I slept well for the first two nights, but on the third night, I couldn't sleep. Queasiness took over my body. And mind. My back hurt. Even though the idea of eating repulsed me, I gorged on food. For the next ten days, I kept eating but barely slept. I sat in front of my computer to write but couldn't string a sentence together. I walked the virgin prairies outside the mansion and cried from exhaustion. Sometimes I screamed. I was at the colony to write, to think, to relax, but instead I felt stupefied and starved.

A fellow resident, a Japanese composer who played the cello, often spoke about the spirit world, so I asked him for advice. He had recently spent time at the Millay Colony in upstate New York. There, after making a snide comment about Edna St. Vincent Millay, a pebble spewed from nowhere and hit his face.

"There is a spirit in your room," he said, the lenses of his black horn-rimmed glasses magnifying his eyes. "This is why you are sick and can't sleep." He told me he saw the spirit when he looked out the window at night from his bedroom. "You're an easy target," he said. "You're too open." He said the spirit entered my body from the back of my neck and tried to synchronize with me. "The spirit is sucking your energy," he said. "You're eating for two." Now, he said, I needed to tell the spirit to go away. "Don't be nice. You're too nice. Be forceful."

That night I sat up in my bed and yelled, "Get the hell out of here and let me sleep! Leave me alone! It's time to move on!" I waved my arms. "You are not fucking welcome here anymore!" I sneered and pointed both index fingers. Within the hour, I fell asleep. When I awoke, I felt great.

At breakfast, the Japanese composer, hunched over and sweaty, asked how I slept. "The spirit," he said, "came to me last night. Because I told you to be forceful, the spirit is very angry. And now I am sick. I didn't sleep." He wiped his forehead. "It's okay," he said. "Only for two more days. Then I go." He rubbed his forehead. "You need to be more discerning," he said. "You are too open but not open enough. You're only 70 percent open. You need to close bad energy out, let good energy in."

Six months later, I pondered his advice when I responded to
OpenWide66's Internet personal ad. She wrote, "I've worked
on myself for the past three years and now I'm open and ready
to meet my match!" She loved dogs, travel, and ethnic food. A
painter and bass guitarist, OpenWide66—Gina—had dark curly
hair and an athletic body, grew up in an Italian family in Boston,
and knew how to cook a mean spaghetti sauce.

We met at a Holiday Inn located in a small college town
between us, making sure to get separate rooms. After I knocked
on her door, she hugged me, invited me in, and began to tap
on a waist-high bongo drum. Her white tank top highlighted
her tanned, muscular arms. We talked about our drives, the
weather, and between her tapping, she ate a piece of cake I
brought. "This is good," she said, her eyes on my shoes. Rarely
did she make eye contact. Rather, she picked up her keys, her
phone, whatever happened to be nearby; like a surveillance
camera, her eyes roamed.

Gina had brought along a cigar box of relics: pieces of old
jugs, plates, arrowheads, bird skulls. "Check this one out," she
said, a jagged stone splayed in her hand. In between each new
relic, I studied Gina, her hands, her teeth. Strong hands. Straight
teeth. From the cigar box she picked up a small antique medicine
bottle. "It's Depression glass," she said. "From the 1920s."

I felt the tiny letters on the dark green bottle. "My mother
collected old bottles," I said. "Carnival glass too."

"I love going into antique shops," she said.

My mother loved going to antique shops too. She'd drag me
from one dark store to the next. The old stuff scared the hell out
of me. I'd cry, plead for my mother to leave. I felt the energy of
old things, the mildewed heaviness of time.

Before we sat down at a café that evening, Gina said, "I need

to face the wall. I'm a very visual person and get distracted easily."
After the meal, she said, "The couple at the next table listened to
us the whole time."

Back in my hotel room, we sat next to each other on my bed.
She showed me old family photos, reddish-brown images of a
young father in swimming trunks, his big hands wrapped around
Gina's five-year-old body, another of Gina and her two brothers in snowsuits, a now long-dead German shepherd in front of
them. Impressed by her yearning to share her family, her passions, I took a liking to Gina. But when I touched her shoulder,
she froze up. She stared at the photos in her hand.

I slowly tugged my arm away.

A minute later, she lay the photos down, put my hand back
on her shoulder, leaned over and kissed me. "I needed to reboot,"
she said.

Before she left my room, we held each other, kissed, laughed
about the supposed spiders and crickets, dead and alive, lingering in each room (according to an online customer review).
Excited about meeting someone who loved to travel, make art,
play music, I could barely sleep that night. In the morning, we ate
steak and eggs at a diner.

Gina and I talked on the phone constantly and visited every
other weekend. We both lived a dream of having found *the one*,
the one who'd put an end to the dating nightmare. We laughed
when meditating upon Dolly Parton's sexuality, when Gina
referred to a party as a "social," when we'd get into the minds of
our dogs (she had three) and improvise dog conversations. She
told my friends she adored me. I told my friends I couldn't imagine not having Gina in my life.

I stepped right into OpenWide66's life, her heart, her psyche.
According to the Japanese composer's openness scale, we both
must have been at least 92 percent open.

One night, a month into our relationship, Gina had an 80s
song going though her head. Before telling me the name, I asked

if I could guess. I put my head against hers and told her to concentrate. A minute later, I said, "Does it have something to do with men?" She moved her head away from mine, squinted her eyes and said, "Men at Work. They sang the song. That song that starts with the lyrics, 'I can't get to sleep.'"

Two months into the relationship, Gina talked about moving to my town and making a life with me. She sent me MLS listings, beautiful old homes with at least an acre of land. I looked forward to building a future with Gina.

But three months into the relationship, Gina phoned me. In a low, monotone voice, as if she just witnessed a gory accident and couldn't make sense of it, she said, "When I feel overwhelmed, I walk through the aisles of Target and look at the merchandise. That's what I did tonight. I felt overwhelmed in my last relationship."

Not sure why she felt this way now, I said, "But we had a great weekend together!"

"I need to buy a day-planner, a calendar," she said. "I have too much to do. I'm tired." Two days later, she brushed off the comments about being overwhelmed. "Things are better now," she said. "I have a calendar."

Although she still cooked gourmet Italian meals for me, recipes from her grandmother's yellowed index cards, I began to feel a fortress around her, a wall made of concrete and lead, the kind surrounding contaminated nuclear reactors. The colony ghost would have had a hard time getting through the back of her concrete neck.

I learned Gina spent a lot of her free time alone, much of it sleeping. She loved to sleep. "It's not depression," she said. "I come from a family of heavy sleepers." Often Gina fell asleep by nine. Out cold.

I also learned she didn't have many friends. Every now and then she ate meals with one friend, a deeply depressed woman who also slept a lot. The few times I met the friend she talked about her awful ex-husband who had left her five years before.

Once Gina commented about the depressed friend, "I don't know much about her life. She's very private. That's why I like her."

Gina prided herself on being private. "Some things should only be discussed," she said, "on a need-to-know basis." She said it wasn't right of me to tell a friend how much I paid for my house.

"It's public record," I said. "Anyone could find out."

Once I told Gina about a good friend who made no secret about the sexual abuse she endured as a child—in fact she spoke to college students about her experiences. Gina shut her eyes and hit her fists against the table. "You shouldn't be telling me this! It's private! Isn't anything sacred?"

I pointed at her. "Too many women keep it a secret because they feel ashamed, like they deserved it."

Silence.

Gina usually walked with her head high, impervious to the outside world, but now her eyes watered.

I held her, kissed her neck.

"I don't cry. I'm usually very strong," she said.

One day Gina stopped the car so we could look at a river. She stared off in the distance, the same expression my mother often had. Now my mother was dead, and Gina sat beside me, a wall between us. "The wall," I said. "When it's up, I feel more alone than when I'm really alone."

"I work really hard to be strong," she said.

"You're too closed," I said.

"You're too open!" she blurted back.

Gina started the car. "Want to go to Dairy Queen?" she asked. Her eyes might have been open to colors and shapes, but her heart couldn't have been, at this point, more than 28 percent open. My openness tumbled down to 46 percent at most.

The first time I tried to leave, I paced outside Gina's house, car keys in hand. She asked what I was doing.

"I'm not happy," I said. "The wall. It makes me so sad. I need to go."

Gina sat on her porch and cried. "Please don't leave," she said. "I don't know how to do this. Relationships. Give me time to learn." I slid the keys back in my pocket and held her. "I need you," she said. "I'll go to therapy."

Gina began to suffer from panic attacks, vertigo, high blood pressure. She blamed her ailments on the silicone earplugs I had given her. After a doctor's visit, she called me. "The doctor thinks it could be related to what I'm talking about in therapy," she said. "This is the first time I feel safe enough to deal with my issues. Knowing you're there to support me."

The second time I tried to leave was after Gina made rules about how we communicate: *Don't leave phone messages for me unless you have something important to say; I could see your missed calls. Don't call back until I call you. I don't want technology in the bedroom so I can't talk to you from bed.*

The third time I tried to leave was right before I took off for a psychic medium course at a spiritual retreat. I wanted to learn the difference, once and for all, between open and too open.

That morning I prepared breakfast for Gina. While gathering butter, eggs, and pancake mix on my counter, I said, "I have this old rock 'n roll song going through my head. Can you guess what it is?"

Gina, sitting at the kitchen table, stomped her foot. "I'm not playing this game anymore!" she said. "This is private stuff. You shouldn't mess with it. Ouija boards aren't cool. You shouldn't mess with the dead."

I stormed out of the kitchen. "I was just trying to connect with you!" I yelled from the hallway.

I've never messed with Ouija boards, or the dead. But the dead messed with me.

Again I told her I needed to break it off, but Gina insisted I give her a chance. "Please," she said, "I'm not used to someone caring about me."

I wanted to believe she could change. But was I only playing out my own childhood issues again and again with one partner after the next? I had begged, over and over, to get my mother's attention, but even after pleading with her, she continued to watch television, study grocery store advertisements, or sing to our poodle. Over and over, I also tried to get Gina to open up, to see me. Why couldn't I just tell her to get the hell out of my life, like I did with the spirit at the art colony?

In the psychic medium class, the teacher asked for brief introductions and why we were taking the class. I told him about my fear of old furniture, how I'd cry when my mother dragged me from one antique shop to the next.

"You're sensitive," he said, "to different energies. You'll learn how to deal with these energies."

The teacher spoke about how our auras are like car windshields—they need to be clean enough to see through but strong enough to keep out the sun, insects, and hail. He spoke about chakras and how to shield ourselves from negative energy. He said it's not only unhappy spirits who prey on open, vulnerable targets. Just like an angry dog, unhappy people also sense vulnerabilities. When they see an opening, they'll attack. He said in order to communicate with others "in this world or on the other side," we need to have an open line.

After the spiritual retreat, I visited Gina. Unconsciously my psyche closed down, but the more shut down I was, the more open Gina became. She looked into my eyes, listened when I talked. Even though she took a break from therapy— she was "sick of analyzing everything"—we held hands while walking through fields of soybeans across from her house. She thanked me for all the love I'd given her. We hugged. Tight. I stroked Gina's hair, kissed her neck.

That evening, we ate at a Vietnamese restaurant. While Gina chewed, she stared at the napkin in front of her, the ceiling, the curtains blocking the sun. I attempted to talk, to connect, to have a conversation, but she kept eating, her eyes fixated on the shrimp dish served at the next table. As if she'd never seen shrimp before. As if the shrimp were telling a fascinating story. On our drive home, I told Gina how uncomfortable I felt, sitting across from her in a restaurant and not talking the entire time.

"I already talked with you today," she said, her eyes on the road. "I needed downtime. I wanted to focus on the food."

The next day, in front of Gina's depressed friend, Gina touched my shoulder. I flinched—an automatic reflex. My body closed down. My body said *enough*. Gina and I both noticed her friend's stunned face: eyes wide, mouth open in an *O*. I squirmed in my seat. Gina closed her eyes, moved her head from side to side. We had a witness.

Perhaps I was too open *for her*. But I'm okay with my open, vulnerable self. Now I'm more mindful of the aura windshield; when it's thick and darkened, nothing can enter or exit. A shield against heartache, yet a shield that shuts out the good stuff like sunlight, love, humanity.

I'm not sure how the Japanese composer came up with my 70 percent openness factor. Can a formula really exist? What I do know, though, is that before I left the art colony, I entered the ghost-room one last time and hoisted up my luggage. Before closing the door, I took a deep breath and said, "Thank you."

30
Dating My Mother

From her blurry photos, Beth looked like my mother: same jawline, same big-toothed smile, same red hair. Over the phone, she sounded like my mother. Beth obsessed about her old, blind tabby, similar to my mother, who obsessed over our blind miniature poodle. Not great attributes, but familiar.

My friends admired me for throwing myself back into the dating pool, for not letting a string of failed relationships stop me from trying again and again. One friend said, "Hope springs eternal." I should have known better: If I got the same results over and over, shouldn't I change my approach? After all, I was the common denominator. But I was the writer, always in search of a good story, an interesting character. No matter the price. At least that's what I told myself.

Soon into our correspondence, Beth, who lived across the country in New Mexico, asked how I felt about sending food back in restaurants. She wrote, "It drove my ex-girlfriend crazy." And I said, "I could understand sending a burger back if it's rare and you wanted it well-done, but it could be a deal breaker if it happens all the time."

Similarly, my mother's restaurant behavior was idiosyncratic. She stuffed breadsticks, jelly, and butter sachets into her purse, and more often then not, studied and recalculated the bill, often pointing out a five-cent discrepancy. At McDonald's, my mother never ordered enough French fries, always ordered three or four for the six of us, and would dump them out and redistribute them. "Oh, they all fell out," she said.

Beth sent more photos, all unclear or from a distance. "Why don't we try to Skype," I said.

"I need to order a special camera," she said. "My computer is too old. Trust me, a lot of women want to date me. My ex of seven years says I'm drop-dead gorgeous."

Beth had another advocate, a woman she met at a bar twenty years before, a woman who could have been her mother. They talked on the phone but seldom spent time together. The advocate left a message for me: "Beth is brilliant and beautiful and a wonderful singer."

"She called you?" Beth asked. "I told her not to."

When I asked how the advocate got my number, Beth had to get off the phone to put her clothes in the dryer.

She told me she sat on a magical rock in the woods and my dead mother came to her and asked her to take care of me. I told myself this woman is crazy. I told myself this woman is not for me. But I wanted to believe her.

She told me about her activist work: "I organized protests against Walmart all over the Southwest." She said she received death threats in the past, "But," she told me, "those big corporations won't stop me."

At the airport, Beth, wearing an army jacket, tight jeans, and red cowboy boots, hugged me. She proceeded to tell me about the bumpy plane ride: "The pilot probably just got his license. The plane went *boom* onto the ground," emphasizing the word "boom" by hitting her knee with her fist. She talked fast. She made me laugh. Tall and skinny, a messy, red bob atop her head, she had striking green eyes, maybe a little too close together. Attractive enough.

Throughout the weekend, I studied Beth's face, her slightly witchy nose. I studied the way she held her fork (in her fist, poking her food as if harpooning a fish). She told me she loved my house, my dog, my friends. At my kitchen table, she talked about her activist work. She told me she had a rare stomach disease. She told me about a poor black girl she befriended when she was in the third grade. "Everyone else

made fun of her," she said. Later, in her tight jeans, she mod-
eled her ass for me. "Nice, huh? All the black men love it." She
looked into my eyes and told me she loved me.

I wasn't sure what to make of that.

One day we walked in the woods, hand in hand, until she
unclasped her grip and ran towards a big tree. "Let's climb it!" she
said. She scaled the trunk and threw her legs and arms around
a big branch until she pulled herself up. "Come on!" she said,
motioning me to join her.

"I'm not that agile," I said.

"You can do it!" she said, petting the branch as if it were a
dog.

I convinced myself Beth understood me. After all, we were
both Jews from the same Russian stock, Jews obsessed with the
Holocaust, Jews who survived dysfunctional families, Jews who
spoke the same language.

I later learned about the lies she told me: that this was her
first foray into Internet dating; that none of her girlfriends ever
wanted to break up with her; that she'd been president of a big
activist organization; that she was a soft drink heiress who'd
ghostwritten a book about a famous dancer, started medical
school but dropped out, and been propositioned by Emmylou
Harris.

My mother also told lies. When I said, "Ugh, there's a beetle
in the chicken soup," my mother scooped the bug up with her
fingernail. "It's just pepper," she said, followed by a flick and a
small chuckle.

A few months before my sixteenth birthday, my mother
organized her own surprise twenty-fifth wedding anniversary
party on the pretense that my siblings and I had planned it for
her. One night at the kitchen table, my brother and I signed
cards and addressed envelopes from a long list of her friends and
relatives. At one point, my mother insisted that I write neater.
On the cards, as my mother instructed, we wrote, "Keep this a

secret! When you call to RSVP, please ask for one of the kids." At the time, I didn't understand why my mother couldn't just throw the party—why did it need to be a surprise that wasn't really a surprise? She even made the decorations—two large cardboard hearts covered with aluminum foil, overlapping, one with the word HAPPY, the other with ANNIVERSARY. When my mother walked into the roomful of guests, she gasped. "Oh my!" she said. "My children are wonderful! I can't understand how they kept this a secret!"

With only a learner's permit in hand, I accidentally hit a parked car outside of Fortunoff's, a department store. My mother, who never got her driver's license, sat in the passenger seat. A minute later, the owner of the dented car walked up to me.

"You just hit my car," she said.

"No she didn't," my mother said.

I stood silent, a turquoise scuff mark from our Impala station wagon on the edge of the dent.

Despite my mother's denial, she sent the woman seventy-five dollars to get the dent knocked out.

Beth told me she had made lots of money selling expensive time-shares to tourists. She told me she was the number one salesper-son for two years. Her advocate later said she worked for less than a year. She had a few good weeks but mostly didn't earn enough to survive; her advocate told me her girlfriend of seven years sup-ported her. When I confronted Beth, when I said, "You need to tell me the truth," she proceeded to read a recommendation letter, written by her girlfriend of seven years, to support her entrance into law school.

We spent three short weekends together before Beth talked about driving to Virginia to see her mother. I invited her to stop by my house along the way. Her stop along the way turned into a plan to stay for two months. Before the visit, she arranged to move out of her apartment, to find something closer to downtown Albuquerque, so, she said, why not put her stuff in storage and save on two months rent? Since she didn't like the storage spaces she found, she said she would rent a U-Haul, drive it across the country, and store her stuff at my house. I told her that was a bad idea. I told her I didn't want all of her stuff at my house. I told her we barely knew each other. And she said, "You know how many women would want to live with me?"

Now a huge (among many) red flag waved in my face. So why couldn't I tell her to go live with one of those many women and be done with her? Maybe it was the writer in me who wanted to see this play out, to prove she was nuts. But by engaging with her, I only proved that I was just as nutty as she was. Yet women, straight and gay, tell me similar stories of how potential partners try to woo them with ego, as opposed to kindness. One friend told me about a suitor who said, "You'll never meet anyone better or smarter than me." The institutional pressure from the media (starting with Disney and most mainstream movies and songs), from religious institutions—pretty much everywhere—sends us the message we should be partnered, and if we're not, there's something terribly wrong. One ex of mine said she'd rather be in a relationship than not be in a relationship. I asked, "Even if the relationship is unhealthy?" She repeated again, "I'd rather be in a relationship than not in a relationship." Enough said.

Beth reminded me I had promised to help her pack. I had already bought the ticket. So I boarded the plane. Maybe out of morbid curiosity. We had six days to pack. She hadn't collected boxes. She hadn't bought packing tape. She hadn't sorted anything out. Her closets were piled high. Clothes and shoes and wood and tools and tennis rackets. "You've got a lot of stuff," I said. Beth hummed and kissed her cat. I lay down and cried.

Beth hoarded her dead uncle's razors, her dead grandfather's golf clubs, bike helmets, colanders, vacuum cleaners, paper placemats.

My mother was a hoarder, too. As a result of double-coupon specials, our basement looked like a stockroom from the supermarket's nonperishable section, including a three-year supply of sanitary napkins, even before I needed to use them. And never mind the two-car garage piled high with old bicycles, baby shoes, and broken shutters.

I packed one hundred and twenty boxes, including all five colanders, while Beth sifted through papers. At one point she asked me to peel the address labels off old magazines, magazines she had planned to throw away. Afterward she found one missed label. "I told you to get all of them!" she said. I told her no one cares about her address, she's moving anyway, and anyone could find her address if they really wanted to. All the while, her blind, shaky cat bumped into boxes, walls, and meowed when we ate. Beth told him to shut up, then threw food for him. "Gives him something to do," she said.

Beth invited a friend over to help her pack. A perky woman who hadn't known Beth long, who said she loved packing. The woman packed her breakables, and I continued to box up everything else. I helped her friend pack a box or two, and Beth walked by. "You're not doing that right!" she screamed in front of her friend, before I could even figure out what dish could fit in which box.

I left the apartment. I walked fast. Faster. I had enough. I called her advocate. Now the advocate was angry at Beth for mistreating me. Now the advocate told me of Beth's exes who ran away, wanting nothing more to do with her. Her advocate said that as far as she knew, Beth never did any activist work; rather she sat at home, talked on the phone, and made lunch for the woman who supported her for seven years. She told me the girlfriend of seven years will never agree to see Beth again, only talk on the phone, because of the unhealthy relationship they had. Her advocate said, "She told me it was Jamie Lee Curtis who came on to her, not Emmylou Harris." Her advocate told me how Beth was looking for someone to support her like her ex of seven years did. Her advocate told me about all the years she cut Beth out of her life, the lies she caught her in, the poetry Beth claimed to have written, but the advocate knew better and confronted her. "Those poems are from Kahlil Gibran's *The Prophet*," she told Beth.

I asked the advocate why she advocated for Beth. "She gave me the impression she was getting better," she said. "I wanted to believe if she met the right person, she'd change her ways."

I bought a plane ticket home. Beth, now pale-faced, her hair matted down, said, "I feel sorry for you because you could have experienced something awesome with me."

Beth insisted on going to a fancy restaurant before I left. She interrogated the waiter about the salmon special. When the salmon arrived, Beth poked her finger in the fish and shook her head. "It feels dry," she said. She asked me to taste it while the waiter stood watching.

"It's fine," I said, staring at the breadbasket.

"You sure?" Beth asked.

"It's *fine*," I said again.

Perhaps Beth did have a rare stomach disease. Besides the thick layer of red smeared across her lips, her ghostly face and vibrant, green eyes faded into sickly shades of gray. I wondered why the scrawny woman in front of me felt the need to impress others with lies. But I didn't need to find out. I needed to walk the hell away.

At that point, I would have slurped up my mother's chicken soup with beetles. I wanted to hug my mother, thank her for the three-year supply of Maxi Pads. She did the best she could. In her twenties, she didn't have a choice. She had to get married and have kids. She had to follow the script set out for her. Relatives told me she was a vibrant teenager, a popular college student who loved all kinds of art. And despite my father's distain for travel, she loved to roam through different parts of the world, a trait I inherited from her.

I breathed deep, ate my salmon, and looked at Beth. She looked nothing like my mother.

31

The Big Smoke

After your last relationship with a pathological liar ends, you're a little weary; maybe your vision's gone fuzzy when it comes to recognizing fatal flaws, or maybe you see a little scrap of love at the end of the tunnel and you're willing to do whatever it takes to get it. Or you're addicted to the attention, the drama, or just afraid to be alone. Or maybe you need more writing material.

So when you receive a personal-ad message from a Canadian brunette, attractive in that Sandra Bullock kind of way, you write back, not concerned about expensive flights or having to go through passport control to meet her. Right now you are hers and she is yours and you exchange e-mails about what makes you cry, and you say beautiful scenery and thinking about your dead mother and stupid romantic comedies, and she says seeing her students confused, then enlightened, when she teaches them about the social construction of gender. You talk about being a New York Jew, how you once heard a poet say, "Jews are like everyone else but more so," and she shoots back, "And WASPs are like everyone else but less so." Despite the fact that she lives in another country, she's everything you're looking for. You meet on Skype and talk and laugh for three hours. You stare at her lips and imagine kissing them. The next morning, she writes, "I'm a little speechless, so I'll just drink my coffee."

You tell your friend about the Canadian, and she says, "Are you crazy? Canada?" And you say, "She lives in Toronto! It's supposed to be a great city!" You tell your therapist about the Canadian and she says, "Do you think you might have intimacy issues, to seek out women from such a distance?" And you say, "Why limit myself? Besides, I can't seem to meet suitable women in this small town." Your therapist crosses her legs and sighs. She says, "Suitable women come to town all the time." You shake your head from side to side and say, "That's because I invite them."

You and the Canadian e-mail daily and Skype often, but there are nights you don't hear from her. Sometimes you receive an e-mail sent at four or five in the morning. Sometimes she slurs her words and jabbers on. One night she tells you she doesn't live in Toronto; rather, she lives in a small nickel-mining town four hours north. This nugget of information doesn't worry you as much as her drinking. You tell her you can't handle alcoholics, you've already had your share, but she insists she doesn't have a problem. She drinks, she tells you, because she's bored, and it's only secondary to hanging out with friends. She says you shouldn't worry; she stays out drinking all night only two or three times a month. She says she doesn't need to drink, she never drinks alone, and she doesn't like to have drunken sex. She asks you, with a confused look on her face, "What's your definition of an alcoholic?" You don't answer. You're pretty sure she's not telling you the truth, but maybe there's not much to do in her small town. Maybe this is what Canadians do.

You fly up to Toronto and she meets you at the airport, where she holds your hand while leading you to her car. You like holding her hand. She looks a bit older in person and you think to yourself, probably from all the drinking, or maybe too many hours in the sun, but you quickly get over the wrinkles and kiss her in your Toronto hotel room, and for the next three days, you stroll arm in arm, eat fancy dinners, and take nighttime walks on the beach. You notice that every chance she can, she works on a crossword puzzle or solving a Sudoku, which she refers to as her other girlfriend. You notice she doesn't look you in the eye when she talks, that she has a tendency to zone out, like your mother.

She orders a few beers at dinner the first two nights, and on the third, you both drink two martinis. You say, "It's getting late, we need to eat." She says, "I could drink all night. I don't need to eat."

After you return home, you have plans to talk on the phone, but she doesn't answer. Two hours later, she calls. She's drunk. It's only courteous to show up for a phone date, you say, especially after spending three days together. She says you should be glad she called at all. You say you don't know if you can do this. You say you feel disrespected. The next day she apologizes, says she will be a better girlfriend. "Have faith in me," she says. "Give me time."

You give her time. After all, she was at a friend's birthday party.

She visits you in Asheville for six days, and for the duration, she has an awful cold. Still, you tour the Biltmore House and hike the Blue Ridge Mountains. While she lay in bed, a stack of tissues by her head, you ask if she wants an old pair of Doc Martens.

"Sure," she says, raising her foot. "Put one on and see if it fits."

It fits perfectly.

"It's like the lesbian Cinderella!" she says.

But you're not sure you're her lesbian prince, especially after you go off to teach a night class and she stays home to prepare a spinach pie. When you return, she says she hasn't eaten anything. You think you might smell alcohol on her breath, but you chalk it up to cough medicine. Later you discover three empty beer bottles in your kitchen pantry.

You both agree the trip went well. "Considering how sick I was," she says, "you were a good sport." She invites you to spend your winter break in her nickel-mining town. You accept.

But before meeting again, she tells you she ignored a student who came to her office to complain about a grade. She tells you she screamed at a workman, called him an idiot and told him to get the hell out. She tells you no one she met on the Internet lasted more than a week at her house.

Your therapist says, "Do you really think you'll escape her wrath?"

"Maybe I should cancel my trip," you say.

"I can see you've already made up your mind," your therapist says. "So have fun. Take notes."

You suspect it's a bad idea to go, but you still hold onto a tiny shred of hope. Maybe she won't need to drink if she's not bored, and of course, she won't be bored with you around. Besides, you need to play this out, finish the story you started. So you travel to her nickel-mining town in the dead of winter. The roads are icy, the sky gray, and the Canadian points out the city's claim to fame, The Super Stack, the tallest chimney in the Western Hemisphere. "We call it 'The Big Cigarette,' or 'The Big Smoke,'" she says. It never takes long to spot the Super Stack, tall as the Empire State Building, looming above the city, dispersing sulfur gases and other byproducts of the smelting process.

The Canadian makes homemade desserts and soups and you spend a lot of time in bed and joke about the book you plan to write together about Internet dating. "We'll reenact profile poses," she says. "Ya know, those shots with people on the phone or standing by their sports car." And you say, "How about a caption of, 'I'm at home in a baseball cap or a burka'?"

So far so good, but on the fourth night, she drinks and drinks and drinks. You watch in disbelief, as she drinks one quart of beer after another. You really don't want to keep track but you notice four, or was it five, empty quart bottles lined up. You don't understand how it's physically possible to drink that much. At least she's a happy drunk. She looks you in the eye. She holds her hand out and you dance, and she likes that you dance and says, "How fun you are! A whole other side I didn't know about!" Another night she drinks beer and champagne and whiskey and more beer and she professes her love to you, says why don't we get married, after all, gay marriage is legal in Canada, but soon after, she passes out. You imagine your wedding reception, an open bar at the local tavern, adjacent to the Super Stack. Later she wakes up, makes pasta in the nude, and passes out again. You ask if she remembers the night. She says, "Don't remember a thing. Tell me about it."

You help her slice apples for a pie, homemade crust and all. Her cat purrs and rubs against your leg, and for a moment, you ignore the drinking. She even stops what she's doing, washes her hands and wraps her arms around you from behind. She kisses your neck, says, "I'm so glad you're here."

To make the piecrust, she uses animal lard, and you pick up the package and say in a joking manner, "It's the poor man's butter." She continues to knead the dough but doesn't say much. Then she accuses you of demoralizing her. "There are consequences to language!" she says. You're not sure how the butter comment is demoralizing, or how language has consequences in regards to pie ingredients. Maybe it's a class issue, but the Canadian grew up solidly middle-class, like yourself.

On New Year's Eve, you stay at the Holiday Inn, a getaway for the night. When you pull into the parking lot, you say, "Maybe we can ask for a top floor, for a quiet room." She snaps back, "What else do you want?" What you want is to ask about language and its consequences, but you keep your mouth shut. Once in the room, she pulls out a crossword puzzle. You take a walk in the bitter cold, past icy parking lots and crowded liquor stores. The Super Stack spews out a purplish-yellow mist. You walk and walk until your nose and cheeks and fingers are frozen, until your lips are blue.

She invites you under the covers, and you watch *The Secret*. There's something to this, you both say, then you both make lists of what you want. She wants someone to offer her a great job without applying for it. "I've always gotten what I've wanted," she says. You say you want to get your book published, but don't say what's next on your list: finding a healthy partner, one who is able to look you in the eye when sober.

The next day, she accuses you of demoralizing her when you ask if she needs her wallet that's sitting on the kitchen table, before you leave to see a film. "If I needed it I'd take it!" she barks.

"There are consequences to language." You're not sure how asking if she needs her wallet is demoralizing, but you apologize for any misunderstanding. You think about leaving. You think maybe she's off her rocker. You think about taking another walk around the block when you return from the movie, but it's fifteen degrees below zero.

You make it through ten of the planned twelve days in this nickel-mining town, where pink granite mountaintops have been stained charcoal black. You make it through the Canadian lashing out several more times and following each incident, she says, "There are consequences to language."

The last time, you respond, "There *are* consequences to language!" You change your plane ticket. You put on layer after layer of clothing and storm outside at night, not concerned about subzero temperatures. You tromp along the street's edges, slipping and sliding, away from snow banks and barreling plows, your face and fingers numbed, the Super Stack now a shadowy gash against the black sky.

You could have predicted all of this before you arrived; you knew the end of the story before it began, but you're a writer, so you say, and perhaps you needed to get the details right.

32

The Woman Who Owned a Place in Flannery O'Connor's Hometown

The woman who owned a place in Flannery O'Connor's hometown wouldn't tell me where she worked. "Maybe," she wrote, "you're one of those liberals who thinks people who work at big corporations are all evil." And I wrote back through the personal ad website, trying my best to sound open-minded, "Big corporations take care of their people, with good insurance and all." I told her about my brother who works for a big corporation and how I didn't have a problem with that, and she finally told me she had a high managerial position with a big box retailer, and I thought, *Well we can't all teach women's studies.* She told me she considered herself a little vanilla, and after dating a pathological liar and a string of alcoholics, I thought maybe a little vanilla might do me good. She asked, "What would you do if you found what you're looking for, if you found someone who could give you what you want?" I told her I'd be thrilled, and when we finally talked on the phone, she went on and on about the corporation, how she'd been there for years, how they treated her well. At least she felt passionate about something, even if it was a big corporation, and she had money and a job and lived in a gigantic Savannah loft and owned a vacation home in Flannery O'Connor's hometown; and she was smart and in shape and maybe I hit the jackpot with this woman, the vanilla corporate Southern woman and I thought vanilla ice cream went well on apple pie because it doesn't overwhelm, not that I'm considering myself anything close to apple pie—after all I'm a New York Jew with neurotic tendencies who prefers chocolate ice cream with almonds or mint.

The woman who owned a place in Flannery O'Connor's hometown offered to drive to my house, and I said, "Okay, after I'm done with my two-week writing residency"; and once I settled into the residency I wrote a lot, and maybe once a day e-mailed a short note to the woman who owned a place in Flannery O'Connor's hometown. I'll call her Wendy. From time to time I'd send her a draft of a poem and she'd give helpful feedback. She sent a bracelet made of beads on a leather band she bought at a street fair, a sweet gesture but it made me a tad uncomfortable—maybe because of the ambivalence I felt about our e-mail courtship, maybe because I'd never dated a corporate woman, maybe because, in fact, she could have been the woman of my dreams and I wouldn't know how to handle it.

Wendy pulled into my driveway and she looked cuter in person than in her online pictures, a dark-haired Jodie Foster, and she hugged me and I gave her a tour of my house, and ten minutes later, in my basement, she asked me to kiss her and I said let's go upstairs where it's not mildewy, and we kissed in my kitchen and it was better than expected, and I showed her around town and we ate sushi and she said, "I could be eating shit right now and I'd be happy." She said she'd get a hotel but in the end she slept with me, only sleeping. She left the next day, but not before brunch and a stroll through the woods, where we walked hand in hand.

The next weekend Wendy came back to accompany me to a friend's wedding and met my friends and talked about the corporation, maybe a little too much, but at least she took pride in her work, and our weekend went as well as it could have, even though Wendy didn't engage much with my friends and felt more comfortable yakking about the corporation. But we laughed a lot and shared stories of our exes, because that's what lesbians do, at least in my experience. Sometimes I write about my exes, and Wendy read a number of my stories and asked to see more.

We woke up in the middle of the night and cooked a frozen pizza and slow-danced to a Marvin Gaye song, and who knew frozen pizza could taste so good at two in the morning? I mentioned my upcoming trip to New York to visit family and Wendy said she could take a few days off and meet up with me and I told her I'd love to show her my old stomping grounds, so in the middle of the night, we made hotel reservations and bought expensive tickets to see a Broadway show.

Before the New York trip, Wendy invited me to her place in Flannery O'Connor's hometown, a town once synonymous with "going crazy," since the town used to house what was officially called a lunatic asylum. She had a week's vacation coming and I could stay the whole week if I wanted, and I said I'd come for part of that time and there I was, in Flannery O'Connor's hometown, and it was hot and muggy and thank god she had air conditioning. Her Doberman pinscher sniffed my border collie mix and Wendy said, "Good thing our dogs get along because you never know with my dog. I spent thousands on a trainer."

For the next three days we prepared delicious meals and snuggled into each other's bodies. We rode in her jet ski and walked the dogs, only in the early morning or when the sun went down. Otherwise it was too hot. But even with the heat, I said I could get used to this life, a life full of good food, good sex, and good company.

On the fourth night in Flannery O'Connor's hometown, we dined at a nice restaurant and all seemed fine until Wendy fell silent, and I asked what was wrong and she said nothing, and on our way back to her house she was still silent, staring straight ahead, and I asked again if anything was wrong and she said nothing, and we stopped off to buy water since we couldn't drink from her tap, and the supermarket lost electricity and all was silent and dim except for generators rattling and we loaded ten water jugs in her car. Back at her house, Wendy stared at me, a stern look on her face, her nostrils flared. She said I wasn't open enough, and I said, "Really?" since most people tell me I'm too open, and that's when a hardbound copy of *Flannery O'Connor's Collected Works* gawked at me from her living room coffee table.

"What's going on?" I asked, now a little scared.

Wendy stormed over to the refrigerator and took out an open bottle of wine and poured herself a glass. "Why did you just sit in the car and not talk?"

"I tried to, but . . ." I said.

As if possessed, she continued to stare, her eyes glazed and popping from her head. She pointed at me. "I'm not sure which is worse! If you write about me or if you don't write about me!"

"I don't understand," I said. "Did I say something to offend you?"

Wendy turned the television on and flipped through the movie channel.

I paced by a big red sofa. "If you don't want me here," I said, "I could leave in the morning."

She stomped her foot and ran towards a guest room. "I knew you'd leave me!" she shouted before slamming the door shut.

Stunned, I hobbled towards the room she was in. "What's going on?" I asked.

"Why did you say you'd leave me?" she yelled through the door. "If you're gonna leave, just leave!"

What happened to the sweet vanilla corporate woman? Maybe I should have left but I was in the middle of nowhere by a man-made lake—probably filled with snakes. And it was close to midnight and the sky was pitch black and Wendy cried from behind a slammed door. I slowly opened the door and asked what was going on but she slammed it shut. "Get the fuck out! Leave!" she said. "I've got issues! I couldn't exactly say that in the personal ad!"

Not only was I in Flannery O'Connor's hometown, now I was stuck in one of her Southern Gothic stories, a story written by a woman who famously said, "Anything that comes out of the South is going to be called grotesque by the northern reader, unless it is grotesque, in which case it is going to be called realistic."

Just then my Yankee reality consisted of pacing through Wendy's house. I called for my dog and found her shaking underneath a bed. Wendy came out of the room and sat in front of the television and watched *Finding Nemo*. I lay down in the bedroom and watched the ceiling fan vibrate, in a state of shock. Even if she described herself as vanilla, I had thought she, the white-bread Southern girl, could be the one, which made me think of fond memories I had of taking a class trip to the Wonder Bread factory in Queens, where I breathed in the smell of warm bread and as souvenirs we all got little loaves, the logo of primary color circles dancing above the words.

Wendy came into the room and apologized. "I don't want you to leave," she said. "Please don't go."

"Have you been to therapy?" I asked.

"Fuck that!" she said, her arms swinging around. "I've been to plenty of therapy and it doesn't do a thing!"

She stomped out of the room. A minute later she came back and asked if I had the bracelet she had sent to me.

I told her I hadn't yet unpacked my bags from the writing residency.

"You didn't like it! Admit it!"

I assured her that it was a very nice bracelet. "I'm sorry I didn't bring it."

"You could give a shit about that bracelet!" she said, tromping from the room.

I continued to watch the ceiling fan vibrate.

Finally she came back into the bedroom, twisted the cap off her bottle of sleeping pills, and placed one on her tongue.

I didn't sleep a wink.

Instead I thought about Flannery O'Connor, who never had a physically intimate relationship with anyone. She grew fond of a Danish book salesman and they met up to discuss philosophy and religion and one night he attempted to kiss her. When asked about this kiss years later, he said, "I had a feeling of kissing a skeleton." Soon after he went back to Denmark and met a woman he would marry. Six months later, after Flannery O'Connor received a letter about his engagement, she wrote the story, "Good Country People." In the story, Manley Pointer, a Bible salesman, tries to kiss Hulga, an atheist philosopher who had never been kissed. But the kiss, in O'Connor's story, "produced the extra surge of adrenaline in the girl that enables one to carry a packed trunk out of a burning house, but in her, the power went at once to the brain."

In the morning, my brain felt numb. Wendy apologized. She told me about her abandonment issues and how her parents never appreciated the gifts she bought for them. She begged me not to leave. She cried. She said it wouldn't happen again.

Too exhausted to move, I thought, how could this woman who had an important job at a corporation behave this way? Maybe this was a freak accident, and they say you can't get struck by lightning twice. Again we cooked meals together, held each other's bodies while floating in the lake, watched documentaries, our dogs close by. She told me she loved me; she told me she wanted to travel to New Zealand with me. I told her I loved her too, but what I didn't say: I was leery of her next move and the idea of getting stuck in New Zealand with her scared the hell out of me. Still, I agreed to meet her in New York.

The first night in Manhattan, Wendy and I walked hand in hand, ate a late dinner at an Indian restaurant where we played footsie. She said, "I'm so lucky to have you," and we walked through the streets of Greenwich Village and stopped for ice cream and we looked into each other's eyes and did a lot of smiling. Sappy but true.

The second night in New York, before leaving to see the Broadway musical, I showed Wendy the bracelet she had bought me. "Look," I said, holding it up. I tried to put it on but the clasp was damaged. She stormed out of the room. She walked ahead of me. Jeez. Here we go. I tried to stop her, to ask what's wrong, but the rage had to run its course. "It's not about you," she said, still walking briskly.

The Times Square neon lights swirled and tumbled and the honking echoed and venders offered "I Love New York" T-shirts, three for ten dollars, and throngs of tourists moved like taffy, slow and thick, and there we were, a woman in a rage and a woman who didn't know what to do with a woman in a rage, and I was hungry so I stopped into a pizzeria to get a slice, and she followed and she got a slice and we sat together, silent. Nothing I could do or say helped, and we found the theatre and sat up in the balcony to see a love story about a vacuum cleaner repairman by day and a musician by night, and he meets another musician and they fall in love and create beautiful music, but I couldn't enjoy the beautiful music because Wendy sat next to me, a low-level rage emanating and all I could do was cry. After the show, we didn't talk about the show, we only walked back to the hotel without saying much, and I was starving but she didn't want to eat. She didn't want to talk. She only wanted to take her sleeping pill. Once again, I didn't sleep, especially in a starved state, next to a passed-out rager.

Just me and thoughts of Flannery O'Connor, a devout Catholic. Maybe she was a repressed lesbian and that's why she put every ounce of her energy into writing. Even on her deathbed. When an acquaintance suggested a lesbian subtext to one of her stories, she responded, "As for lesbianism, I regard that as any other form of uncleanness."

At that moment I felt unclean. I knew the healthiest thing would have been to get another hotel room, but it was late and again I was too exhausted, and the next day Wendy asked if I

was going to leave and I said no, even though I knew I would.
I'd be crazier than her if I didn't, but I needed to keep the
peace for another day—fake it 'til you make it. I didn't have the
strength to change flights and hotels, and I could have gone
to my father's apartment on Long Island but then I'd have to
explain the situation and that would have been worse, to explain
to my father about the corporate executive who raged at me in
Times Square, so we took the Staten Island Ferry and ate borsht
at my favorite Ukrainian diner, and that evening something
else set Wendy off, I'm not sure what, but this time she caught
herself and walked up and down thirty flights of steps in our
hotel stairwell, and she came back sweaty and huffing and said
she felt better.

I arrived home and told Wendy this couldn't go on, I didn't
deserve to be treated this way. "You raged at me," I said. "You
scared me."

    She agreed, no I didn't deserve that, but she would change,
she'd already started therapy, she now had a wonderful therapist
and a word for her problem.

    "Have you raged at your other girlfriends?" I asked.

    "Please," she said, "give me a chance." She offered to pay for
both of us to take a workshop for couples, to learn how to get
the love we want, to get the tools necessary to understand our
childhoods and how they led us into our current situation, and
I agreed we both had less than stellar childhoods but still didn't
want to take the workshop; we hadn't been together long enough
to establish a foundation and whatever foundation we did establish was now made of quicksand. I told her I needed space, to not
contact me for at least a month. A friend of mine commented,
"You didn't dodge a bullet. You dodged a cannonball."

Now Wendy is on a spiritual path. She meditates. She goes to
therapy. Over a year later, she told me how our relationship

helped her get to where she is, how grateful she is to me for coming into her life. Perhaps I was the first person to confront her rage head on, although I can't fathom how other girlfriends could have swept the rage under the rug. Maybe they did. After all, Southerners aren't known for their directness.

In Flannery O'Connor's short story, "Good Country People," Hulga, the atheist Ph.D., an expert in nothingness, tries to trick the "simple" Bible salesman by seducing him, but instead, he seduces her by claiming he's sick and going to die. He convinces her to let her guard down and proceeds to steal her wooden leg and eyeglasses and opens up his hollowed-out Bible to reveal condoms and whiskey and sex cards, and he tells her he collects prostheses from disabled people, leaving Hulga stranded in the loft of a barn, where she experiences "a moment of grace," a moment to reassess her arrogance and assumptions.

Wendy asked me to forgive her, saying now she understands the connection between aggression and self-hate. I did. She helped me reassess the emptiness inside of me, the void I had sought to fill by accepting the unacceptable in exchange for a few scraps of love, or the illusion of love—my own hollowed-out bible. And she helped me recognize my own moment of grace. Sometimes it's as simple as getting the hell away.

Epilogue (2014)

And the day came when the risk to remain tight in a bud was
more painful than the risk it took to blossom.

—Anais Nin

This year I delivered the keynote address at my university's
Lavender Graduation, a ceremony to honor the graduating
LGBT students. I emphasized how times have changed since
my college days, how gay marriage was not even a concept
back then, let alone a law to vote for or against. Now gay marriage is legal in a number of states and, like dominoes, addi-
tional states are certain to follow. The issue of gay marriage
has helped normalize the LGBT population, demonstrating
to the mainstream that love is love, no matter the gender. As
more folks come out, as more families and friends can see
there's nothing to fear, acceptance of these once "freaks" and
"sinners" is strengthening; a recent Pew Research Poll showed
that among eighteen to thirty-two year olds, support for
same-sex marriage is at an all-time high of 70 percent. Even
Charles Cooper, the lawyer who argued before the Supreme
Court in defense of California's Proposition 8 that banned gay
marriage, had to reconsider the issue when he discovered his
daughter had made plans to marry her partner in Massachusetts. In a statement to the Associated Press, Cooper said, "My
daughter Ashley's path in life has led her to happiness with a
lovely young woman named Casey, and our family and Casey's
family are looking forward to celebrating their marriage in
just a few weeks."

What I didn't say is that this normalization and acceptance
is about committing to a long-term partnership, about finding
a mate for life. I fully support the right to marry, and one day I
just might take the plunge. We might not be considered freaks

anymore by a majority of the mainstream, but single people, straight or otherwise, still might be considered a threat, a wild card. A case in point: Before a faculty party, a colleague asked, "Who are you bringing to the party?" At the time, everyone in my department was partnered; instead of going alone and being okay, I asked a friend to come along. In hindsight, I didn't want to make my colleague uncomfortable. Her partner and I got along well and, I suspect, my colleague felt threatened to see us chatting together. I know, ridiculous. And enabling another's fear doesn't help anyone.

As a child, the only unmarried adult I knew was my Aunt Irene. Even after her death, relatives bandied about scornful comments because of her unmarried status. The bottom line—single people were loners and unlovable. So if I happened to be single, I had better look for a partner in my waking hours. Or at least that idea had been drilled into me. And is drilled into me on a daily basis.

Often I receive junk mail from insurance companies. On the envelope of one, in bold letters: "Who Will Pay For Your Grave-side Memorial?" Another screams, "How Will Your Family Pay Your Mortgage When You're Gone?" I've ripped these pieces of junk mail up and muttered, "Screw You!" These are subtle, or not so subtle, cues in our culture of fear—get and stay with someone or you will die alone. This is how I interpreted these pieces of junk mail through my own skewed lens. Of course these companies are out to make money and don't give a damn about families.

My keynote speech felt like a coming out celebration for me, a chance to be a strong and confident role model. A number of my friends, and even a smattering of straight students, showed up to support me. Who knew my once-closeted self, the person who lied and evaded the truth about her sexuality, who hated herself and popped her dead grandmother's Xanax to get to sleep, would be telling her "inspirational" story to a roomful of graduating college students ready to step out into the world?

I mentioned a graduating senior who had asked for any advice I could offer her, helpful hints for the real world. I gave her a list of three things: Travel, take risks, follow your heart. The list is interchangeable.

Traveling to a foreign destination—not necessarily via plane, but moving away from your comfort zone, throwing yourself into a new situation, a place of discomfort—opens you up to new possibilities to reinvent yourself. At twenty-two, I signed up for a dirt-cheap British Communist package tour to China. Just broken up with my boyfriend, feeling soulless about my career path, I saved up money, quit my job, sublet my Manhattan apartment for four months, and boarded a flight to Amsterdam. On my own. Fearless. My father asked over and over, "What are you running away from?" Perhaps I was running away from a place of dissatisfaction, of mediocrity. I wanted more to life than just to get by. Didn't I deserve this? Don't we all? In Europe I discovered my love of women, of writing, of feminism. Sassy and adventurous, I followed my heart. I had faith things would work out. But I was also practical. Young, white, and educated, I knew I could get another job when I got back to New York and could save up money if I wanted to do it again. And I did.

At times, instead of following my heart, I followed my fear. Fear of being alone. Fear of never finding anyone. Fear of not being good enough. Of believing I deserved nothing more than scraps. I followed my fear when I found myself in similar situations over and over. As if every relationship represented a different house, a flammable house without a foundation, I walked through each door, ignoring the smell of smoke, the little flames in the corner. Yet in those houses, I saw the mirrors, the mirror reflecting myself, my vulnerabilities, my destructive patterns. I chose to look away. Each house would inevitably burn down, some quicker than others. And when the house went up in flames, so did I. A disappearing act. But somehow, magically, I reappeared. Most times stronger, more resilient, sometimes more fire-retardant.

In reality, when I followed my heart, I followed my gut, my genie in a bottle. I put one foot in front of the other, even if I could only see a couple feet in front of me and trusted I'd make my way home safely. When I already believed the world was mine to explore, whether through writing, love, or a foreign land, magic happened.

Maybe that mawkish movie about the laws of attraction and positive thinking, *The Secret*, rubbed off on me. Like I did when I focused with all of my might during the "psychic game," when my sister and I guessed ten cards in a row correctly, now I can focus on stepping from my trap door, on staying away from the box that has confined me. I can focus on recreating myself through writing, through music, through teaching, through nurturing myself, my community, with or without a partner. After all, I am a magician. I have the ability to create magic. We all do.

About the Author

Photo by Leah Shapiro

Lori Horvitz's writing has appeared in a variety of journals and anthologies, including *South Dakota Review*, *Southeast Review*, *Hotel Amerika*, and *Chattahoochee Review*. She has been awarded writing fellowships from Yaddo, Ragdale, Cottages at Hedgebrook, Virginia Center for the Creative Arts, and Blue Mountain Center. A professor of literature and language at UNC Asheville, Horvitz also directs the Women, Gender, and Sexuality Studies Program. She received a PhD in English from SUNY at Albany and an MFA in creative writing from Brooklyn College.